Sunday Sews

20 INSPIRED WEEKEND PROJECTS

THERESA GONZALEZ

Photographs by NICOLE HILL GERULAT

CHRONICLE BOOKS

SAN FRANCISCO

Text copyright © 2016 by Theresa Gonzalez
Photographs copyright © 2016 by Nicole Hill Gerulat

Library of Congress Cataloging-in-Publication Data available.

ISBN 978-1-4521-3868-8

Manufactured in China

Design by Jennifer Tolo Pierce

Wonder Tape is a registered trademark of Ranger Industries, Inc.

10 9 8 7 6 5 4 3 2 1

Chronicle Books LLC
680 Second Street
San Francisco, California 94107
www.chroniclebooks.com

To Matilda

CONTENTS

INTRODUCTION

IS IT SUNDAY YET?

You may have picked up this book for many reasons: you were drawn to the cover project and needed the instructions to make it. You are learning to sew and seeking out simple, modern patterns for the season. You were inspired by the clean design and photography. Whatever your reason, welcome! I'm happy to have you here.

Inside, you'll find twenty sewing patterns that you can make, modify, embellish, and share in a day or two, depending on your skill level. For beginners, I provide plenty of guidance and instruction to lead you through every project. For intermediate to advanced sewers, you may find these patterns on the easy side but definitely not boring to sew. The timeless silhouettes lend themselves to a wearable collection you'll want to keep for years to come—just freshen up the patterns with new fabrics as you go.

Why Sunday? Well, it's that day of leisure when you do what you will, whether your routine involves a city brunch with friends, services with family, a lazy day with your love, or time for yourself to be creative. You're well rested from a busy workweek by now and have more time to focus on your craft. After all, no matter how basic the project, sewing requires patience and precision—a tired sewer likely won't produce the best results (as I've learned . . .). I also prefer to sew in daylight—with pins and stitching in clear view—and blocking time on a Sunday in a clean house (or at least tidy craft room) sets you up in ideal surroundings to construct a project that you absolutely love.

Inspired by the day of the week, I designed the garments and accessories by the activities in which you may be involved on your weekend, from an easy-to-wear Weekend Wrap Dress (page 49) that you simply slip over and tie at the waist to an Errands Bag (page 125) to tote along to your local farmers' market or favorite shopping district. While many of the designs are fashion projects, you'll also find gift items to give at baby showers and birthdays. Along the way, pick up lessons like machine-stitching buttonholes, installing lapped and exposed zippers, working with rivets and leather straps, as well as shaping your garments with darts and pleats.

Flip to the back of the book to find the pattern and instructions for the Lazy Day Skirt project on page 98. To get more mileage from the patterns, including making them for yourself and for someone else in a different size, check out page 19 for instructions on tracing patterns. The remaining project patterns in this book can be downloaded from www.chroniclebooks.com/sundaysews.

Lastly, please share your work-in-progress as well as your completed projects on Instagram and Twitter using #sundaysewsbook so we can all share successes and roadblocks along the way. Thanks to the wonders of social media, sewing no longer has to be a solitary craft, as I suggest in my acknowledgments. To that end, I look forward to catching up with all of you in the virtual craft space—every Sunday.

Enjoy,

Theresa

PART I: Sewing Techniques

THE BASICS

ABOUT FABRIC

The right or wrong fabric can make or break a project. Imagine a drapey dress made in lightweight linen. Now imagine the same dress in heavyweight denim; it simply won't have the right look or feel. The denim would be a better choice for a tote or an apron where its sturdiness is an asset. Fabric choice makes a significant difference in both the wearability of your finished project and your sewing experience. When I designed the projects in this book, I paired a specific fabric with each one—mostly light- to medium-weight cottons and linens in classic prints. Because they are so easy to sew and wear, I think they are perfect for the stylishly simple projects that you'll find in this book. For the best results I recommend using the fabric suggested, especially the first time you make a given project.

FIBERS

Cotton

Cotton is a great fabric for beginner sewers. It's relatively inexpensive, so if you make mistakes you're not out of a lot of money. It's a strong fabric that doesn't stretch, which means it's less likely to snag, and is machine washable, comfortable to wear, and comes in many great prints. It's also available in a variety of weights and weaves—from shirting (used in the Pixie Dress on page 42) to chambray, corduroy, organdy, and more.

Linen

Linen is a natural fiber that's sourced from the flax plant. It's even stronger than cotton, so you can expect less wear and tear over time. Like cotton, linen comes in many weights and textures, from chambray to twill to shirting. Heavyweight linens are recommended for home décor projects and light- to medium-weight materials for your fashion projects. Before choosing a linen, test the fabric's hand (meaning the weight and feel of the fabric) against your skin to make sure it's right for the project you plan to make.

ANATOMY

Before you start cutting your fabric, take note of its specific make-up. First, see Figure 1 and get acquainted with the key terms. The word *grain*, which you'll see on pattern pieces and in project instructions, is the direction the threads run through the fabric. The lengthwise grain runs parallel to the selvage edge of the fabric. The selvage is the fabric's prefinished (uncut) edge—you'll often see the fabric details printed on it. These are the longest and strongest threads. The crosswise grain runs from selvage to selvage. When you lay out the pattern pieces, you'll want to line them up with the fabric's grain lines—usually with the lengthwise grain of the fabric—to prevent puckering and unflattering shapes in the final garment. On pieces where this matters, you'll see a long arrow printed on the pattern piece to indicate how to orient the paper on the fabric.

When a project or pattern says Right side of fabric, it's referring to the side of the fabric you want to show in the finished project. The Wrong side is the side you don't want to show. In a printed cotton fabric, you'll find that it's pretty obvious which is the Right side and which is the Wrong side. (Most cottons are rolled on the bolt—that is, the large roll you'll see at fabric stores—with the Right side facing out.) If you're working with a solid-colored fabric, be sure to mark the Right and Wrong side so you'll know which is which when you're cutting out your fabric. Mistaking the two can create a noticeable difference in your final garment, and can ruin the outcome. If you're unsure of what the fabric's Right side is, just choose which side you like best and mark that side as the Right side throughout using a marking tool such as a chalk marking pencil or water-soluble pen (see Marking Tools, page 13).

I use nondirectional patterned fabrics for all but one project. Nondirectional fabrics feature prints that look the same when placed upside down as they do when right-side up (such as stripes, plaids, circles) and therefore are easy for beginner sewers to use.

The Matilda Dress on page 65 is the one project that does not feature a fabric with a nondirectional pattern. The fabric in that project has a directional print. Note how the print features an arrow motif, and how the fabric was cut

Figure 1

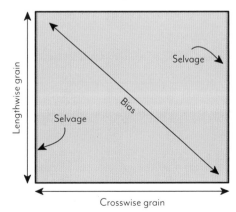

THE BASICS

so the arrows point upward along the vertical centerline of the dress. When creating this dress or any garment using a directional patterned fabric, make sure to cut the pattern pieces from the fabric so the front and back pieces match. The cutting layout for the Matilda Dress lays out the pattern pieces in the same direction to ensure this.

Many cutting layouts in this book, however, instruct you to place pattern pieces on the fabric in opposite directions, which makes the best use of space and reduces fabric waste. This is fine for the nondirectional prints used in this book. If you'd prefer to use a directional print fabric, you will need to alter the cutting layout in order to cut out pieces that match. I've noted the projects in which you will need to alter the cutting layout. In these cases, carefully choose the direction in which you'd like to see your print on the finished project, and note that changing the cutting layout might require more fabric.

PREPPING

Before beginning a project, you should prewash a fabric that is machine washable—especially cotton and linen— as it will likely shrink during the first washing and drying. Launder the fabric as you'd launder the garment. You can often find care instructions on the fabric bolt's label. Jot down any available details about the fabric before you leave the fabric store! Once the fabric is dry, press out any wrinkles with an iron at the recommended setting.

Press your fabric often, before, during, and after you begin a project, for a final look that's more designer than DIY. Keep your ironing board nearby with your iron on the appropriate setting for your fabric (high for cottons and linens). Pressing not only keeps wrinkles at bay (wrinkles sewn into your project can ruin the final result), but also helps open seams and mold your fabrics around curves and corners, all of which will lead to more professional results. Keep your project neat and tidy by trimming away any dangling threads as you work.

INTERFACING AND FACINGS

Some fabrics don't have enough weight or stability to withstand long-term wear and tear. These fabrics need a little help from a friend called interfacing. Interfacing is another layer of fabric that reinforces certain areas of the finished garment like collars and waistbands. Facings, on the other hand, are extra layers of fabric sewn to the wrong side or edge of your project to create a neat finish. Facings are usually made from the same fabric as the garment (also known as self facing). Sometimes you attach interfacing to your facing to help keep those edges neat and provide the structure your garment needs. But don't worry—it's not as complicated as it sounds!

Interfacing comes in woven, nonwoven, and knit varieties. Sew-in interfacing has to be sewn onto the fabric, while fusible interfacing—my preference—

can simply be ironed onto the fabric. Choose an interfacing that's similar to your fabric in weight and weave, and consult the project instructions for details on how you should cut it—for example, on the fold, on a stable grain line, or on the bias (which is the 45-degree angle that crosses from one selvage to the other, see Figure 1, page 11). Be sure to read the interfacing's instructions for prewashing, fusing time, and fusing temperature before using.

YOUR SEWING KIT

Sewing can be an expensive hobby. A wide range of tools are available for every possible task, but *Sunday Sews* keeps it simple. Here are some essential tools (see Figure 2, page 15) to supplement your sewing machine, plus a few nice-to-haves (see Figure 3, page 16) to pick up along the way.

MUST-HAVES

1. Iron and Board

As I mentioned earlier, an iron not only presses out wrinkles, but it also helps mold your project into something that looks professionally made. Invest in a high-quality iron with a steam function, and station it near your sewing workspace. Keep it set at the recommended temperature for the fabric you're working with, so it's easy to press while you work.

2. Shears

Seek out a good pair of dressmaker's shears and designate them for fabric cutting only. You'll also want a pair of medium sewing scissors for cutting curves and trims. A small pair of scissors (like embroidery scissors or metal nippers) are great for buttonholes, detail work, and removing extra threads. Pinking shears, which cut a zigzag edge, are an easy way to finish raw edges so that they don't fray.

3. Ruler

A clear, gridded, 12- to 18-in/30- to 45-cm–long ruler is especially helpful for making 90-degree angles and determining your bias. Make sure that it is clearly marked to $1/8$ in/2.5 mm to mark edge stitching and take other small measurements.

4. Measuring Tape

A 60 in/150 cm flexible measuring tape is useful for determining body measurements for pattern sizing.

5. Marking Tools

Patterns have construction lines and symbols that you'll need to transfer to your fabric pattern pieces—for example, notches that need to line up on the sleeve and the armhole. Chalk marking pencils, available in craft and fabric stores, are easy to use and wash off cleanly from most fabrics. Water-soluble pens meant for fabric work the same way. Air-soluble pens, or disappearing ink, are great if you plan to stitch within an hour or so; if you wait any longer, the marking will disappear. Before beginning a project, test your marking tool on a scrap of your chosen fabric to ensure that it indeed washes off and doesn't show through to the Right side. Since you're washing your fabrics before you start sewing, remember to draw something with your marker or pencil on the Wrong side of the fabric in an inconspicuous place before you throw it in the washer. This will give you the information you need when you're ready to start laying out your pieces!

In the next section, I'll show you how to use markers or pencils with your pins to make your markings. You can also mark your pattern notations onto your fabric using a tracing wheel and tracing paper, which acts like carbon paper. I'll go over that, too.

6. Pattern-Tracing Paper
Have a roll of pattern paper or other semitransparent paper on hand (tracing or tissue paper, for example) to trace the project pattern in this book onto a clean sheet. This will allow you to keep the pattern intact for future use.

7. Pins and Needles
Classic straight pins (or dressmaker's pins) are commonly used for tailoring because they keep fabric secure and flat, which is especially helpful when shaping tricky areas like armholes. Ball-head

pins are ideal for pinning and cutting out pattern pieces. They are also commonly used for home decoration projects that usually require bulkier fabrics. It's a good idea to have both dressmaker's pins and ball-head pins in your kit.

A set of hand-sewing needles comes in handy for sewing hems or buttons and working a temporary stitch or two (also known as hand-tacking). Also, keep an extra set of machine needles on hand in case one breaks. Replace the needle in your sewing machine every time—or at least every other time!—you start a new project. Dull needles lead to tangled threads and jammed bobbins, so this small caution can save you lots of frustration. Be sure to use a needle size that is appropriate for the fabric, such as an 80/12 needle for medium-weight cotton or linen. Most needle packages are labeled to indicate what needle is most appropriate for the fabric you've chosen.

8. Thread
Look for a durable multipurpose polyester or cotton thread when working with cotton and linen fabrics. The thread you choose should be the same color or slightly darker than the fabric you'll be using; for a multicolor fabric, choose a thread color to match the dominant color. When working topstitching meant to show on the Right side of the project, you can opt for a contrasting color as a punchy design feature.

{ Figure 2 }

{Figure 3}

9. Seam Ripper

We all make mistakes, even the experts. Keep a seam ripper on hand to carefully remove bad stitches or when the time comes to remove basting stitches. You can also use your seam ripper to open buttonholes (see page 36).

10. Bodkin

I didn't have one of these for a long time, but I'm including it in the "must-haves" because you'll find it useful in some of these projects, such as the Weekend Wrap Dress on page 49, and they're fairly inexpensive. Used like a large sewing needle, a bodkin makes it easy to pull ribbon, elastic, or a drawstring through a casing. If you don't have a bodkin, you can use a large safety pin instead, but you'll need more patience. The bodkin makes it easy.

NICE-TO-HAVES

1. Awl

This pointy tool allows you to pierce holes through heavyweight fabrics. For instance, an awl will help you insert the rivets in the leather strap of the Errands Bag on page 125.

2. Cover Button Kit

Fabric-covered buttons, used for the Picnic Tee on page 71, are a fun way to embellish jackets, skirts, and cardigans. You can buy kits that contain an easy-to-use tool that presses your fabric right over the button and seals it with a back plate and shank in just one click. Covered buttons are washable, too!

3. Fabric Weights

Place these on top of your neatly laid-out fabric and pattern pieces to keep them in place while you're cutting them out. If you don't have fabric weights, use something small and heavy, like a paperweight.

4. Hook-and-Eye Closures

These small wire hooks, shaped into two decorative loops, are used to secure your garments together. You'll use a set in the Lawn Party Skirt on page 116 to secure the waistband at the top of the zipper closure.

5. Magnetic Pincushion

As much as I love my old-school tomato cushion, a magnetic pin holder holds tight to pins that otherwise might end up on the floor (and in your feet!). Keep one by your machine to pick up pins while you work—it makes cleanup easy.

6. Plastic Canvas

This lightweight plastic comes in a gridded panel and is often used in needlepoint. You'll find it useful for making three-dimensional projects, too, like the Spring Clean Tote on page 130. You'll simply slide this canvas between your fabric and lining at the base of the bag (even the sides if you choose) to reinforce its stability.

7. Pressing Ham

In addition to your everyday ironing board, you'll appreciate having a pressing ham, which makes it easy to iron hard-to-reach places like collars and sleeves, and helps mold tricky curved seams.

8. Point Turner

The pointed end of this small, inexpensive tool lets you poke corners out to the Right side of a project, when turning corners, like in the Baby Gift Set blanket on page 156, while its rounded end helps smooth out curves and seams. If you don't have a point turner, use a knitting needle, pencil, or any other pointy tool.

9. Rivets

These round metal fasteners are used in the Errands Bag on page 125 to secure the leather straps. As you would close up a stud earring, you connect the front piece and back piece together through the hole made by your awl. Then hammer it down to lock it in place on a durable, secure surface that is protected with some kind of padding. Sometimes you want to show off your rivets; for example, the antique-bronze-finish ones used on the bag add a decorative detail on the finished side.

10. Rotary Cutter and Mat

A rotary cutter works like a pizza cutter to quickly slice long lines, making the process of cutting out pattern pieces much easier. But be careful not to slice into the pattern area that should not be cut; this will damage the fabric. Use a flat-edge ruler to guide the cutter along straight lines. A cutting mat is essential with this tool to keep the blade sharp and your table protected.

11. Sewing Gauge

A sewing gauge is handy for measuring small areas, like hems and seams. You can set the guide to a desired length, such as the length of the hem, and check it to ensure that the hem is even throughout.

12. Wonder Tape

Wonder Tape indeed! I love this stuff. It works like double-sided tape to hold two fabrics together, allowing you to keep fabric in place while you stitch, and it comes right off in the first wash. Use it to keep hems even and to hold zippers straight while you sew.

PATTERN PLAY

It's tempting to start cutting out the pattern pieces before reading the instructions, but you don't want to make mistakes before you've even started the project. Prevent any surprises by reviewing the project's step-by-step instructions, as well as the Pattern Legend on page 25, so you know exactly what to expect. Also, note the following Instruction Legend that details how to interpret the figures in each pattern. In the following section, I walk you through sewing pattern basics, including how to follow a project pattern plus additional information that's helpful to know before you get started.

Instruction Legend

Fabric Right side

Fabric Wrong side

Interfacing

---------------- Stitching line

wwwwwwwwwwww Zigzag stitching

— — — — — — Basting

— — —— — · · — Marking or cutting line

MEASURING UP

The fashion sizes in this book range from extra-small to large. Corresponding measurements are outlined in the Size Chart.

To determine your measurements, have someone measure you using your 60 in/150 cm measuring tape. Don't try doing it yourself because your positioning won't be correct, and wear only your undergarments or a swimsuit to get the most accurate fit. To measure the bust, stand up straight, relax your arms along your sides, and have a friend wrap the tape around the widest part of your bust line (which will ensure the most comfortable fit), starting on your back, then going under your arms, then around your bust line to the starting point. When measuring the waist, line up the tape with the smallest part of your natural waist. (And don't suck in your belly when measuring—you want the garment to fit comfortably before and after lunch!) To measure the hips, line up the tape with the fullest part of your hips.

Figure 4

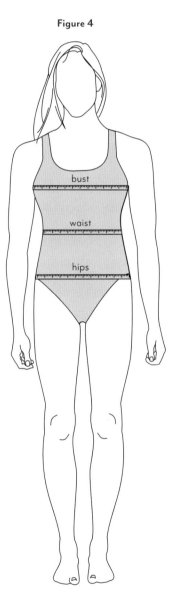

SIZE CHART

Size	Bust	Waist	Hip
XS	31 in/79 cm	25½ in/65 cm	34½ in/88 cm
S	33 in/84 cm	27½ in/70 cm	36½ in/93 cm
M	35 in/89 cm	29½ in/75 cm	38½ in/98 cm
L	37 in/94 cm	31½ in/80 cm	40½ in/103 cm

Follow along the Size Chart and diagram (see Figure 4, page 20) to note all of your measurements. Your body likely won't match up perfectly to one size, so approach it according to what you're making—for example, use your bust measurement for dresses and tops and your hip measurement for skirts.

YARDAGE

Once you know your size, you can determine how much fabric yardage is needed for the project in that size. For example, size Small in the Weekend Wrap Dress requires 2¾ yd/2.5 m of 45-in/115-cm-wide fabric. The width of your fabric will help determine the length you want to purchase and also how you lay out the pattern pieces on the fabric. (A Cutting Layout diagram is included with each project to guide you, using the suggested width fabric.) Most quilting and shirting cottons are about 45 in/115 cm wide. When purchasing fabric, purchase slightly more than called for in the instructions (increase the length ⅛ to ¼ yd/10 to 25 cm) to accommodate for shrinkage when prewashing.

TRACING A PATTERN

As I mentioned earlier, you can trace this book's pattern pieces onto another sheet of paper in order to preserve the original. This will enable you to remake the pattern in another fabric, or make one for a friend in a different size. To do so, you'll need a roll of tracing paper, removable tape, a pencil, and a ruler.

On a flat surface, tape down the original pattern pieces, Right side up. Lay your tracing paper over the pattern and tape it down as well (or use your fabric weights), making sure it is completely flat and wrinkle-free. If it needs smoothing out, you can run an iron across it, choosing the lowest setting. Using your pencil and ruler, trace along your size line and any markings, such as darts, pleats, and seam attachment points, as well as any notes about the individual pattern piece. For curves, which don't allow you to use your straight ruler, work slowly to trace free-hand (start by marking dots along the curve and then join them), or use a French curve, which is a template with several curves of varying radii.

MUSLIN MOCKUP

Before making a project using your chosen fabric, it's a good idea to make a muslin version, using inexpensive muslin purchased in the same yardage as the final fabric. You can try on the muslin garment for size and make any alterations to your pattern pieces (adding or removing 1 in/2.5 cm here or there) to get the perfect fit. Take shortcuts when making the muslin version, by not adding interfacing, not finishing seams, not making buttonholes, and so on. Make the muslin version a day or just before you attempt the project, so that the process is fresh in your mind.

CUTTING YOUR FABRIC

Before grabbing your scissors, lay your fabric on a flat surface, such as a craft or dining table. Fold in half lengthwise (remember, this is the direction of your selvage), with Right sides together and selvages matching, then press. Place the folded edge in the same direction as shown on the Cutting Layout. (Note in a few special cases you'll fold the fabric in half crosswise, which the project instructions will specify.)

Now, look at the Cutting Layout to see how to lay out the numbered pattern pieces on the fabric; make sure to note which piece is which (back, front, etc.). Note that any solid, arrowed lines that say "Place on Fold" should line up on the fold of the fabric. You will not cut on this fold line, as the pattern piece only accounts for half of the full piece.

If your pattern pieces are wrinkled so that they won't lie flat, run your iron, on the lowest setting, over your pattern pieces and fabric. You want to make sure you have an accurate cut, so flat pattern pieces are important.

Now pin or weight down the pattern and fabric, inside the cutting line of your size (see the Size Legend on page 25). Use your dressmaker's shears or rotary cutter to cut as close to the cut line as possible without cutting into it, pressing your hand firmly on the pattern piece to keep it flat. Use your medium scissors to cut around curves. Do not cut out the darts, pleat lines, hem fold, or anything in the center just yet—you'll mark these soon.

Figure 5

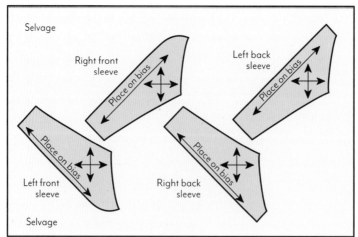

CUTTING ON THE BIAS

Pattern pieces that appear on the Cutting Layout at a diagonal are meant to be cut on the bias. (Fabric cut on the bias will stretch more easily, and is more suited for curved areas like armholes and collars.) Place these pieces on the fabric at a 45-degree angle to the grain line, using your ruler to gauge the degree. Note the cross-shaped directional arrows on the pattern pieces. These help to ensure that you have placed the pattern pieces exactly diagonal to the fabric grain line (see Figure 5, page 22).

Line up your see-through ruler with the edge of the fabric and move the ruler over the cross-shaped directional arrows to line up the pattern piece at a 45-degree angle. If you don't have a ruler that shows a 45-degree angle, simply bring the corner of your fabric toward the opposite selvage so the sides meet and mark that angle by pressing with your iron (see Figure 6).

HOW TO TRANSFER MARKS

The pattern pieces include other helpful symbols that you will mark on your fabric, such as darts and seam attachment points. Look up each symbol on the Pattern Legend on page 25 to determine what it means. Mark these symbols on the Wrong side of your fabric with the pattern still pinned onto it.

Starting at the top of your first piece, use straight pins to mark lines (darts and pleats, for example) and notches (gather points and buttonholes, for example) through both layers of the fabric, especially the beginning and end points. Lift the pattern carefully away, over the pin heads, and draw a

Figure 6

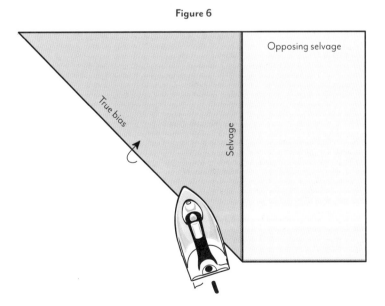

True bias

Selvage

Opposing selvage

line or dot along the pin points, on both Wrong sides, using a ruler when necessary and your marking tool of choice (see Figure 7).

If you opt for a tracing wheel and carbon paper, which can come in sets at your sewing store, starting at the top of the first pattern piece, place your tracing paper between the Wrong side of the fabric and the paper pattern, with the carbon side facing the fabric. Use your tracing wheel to mark lines (darts, pleats, gather points, for example) onto the fabric. Repeat on the opposite side of the fabric by moving the carbon paper to the other Wrong side of the fabric piece (the non-pinned side) and retracing the marking.

Notches tell you where to match up points in the project, such as matching a sleeve to an armhole, as well as showing zipper placement. They're represented on the pattern pieces as small Ts. To mark these, use your small scissors to make a small cut into your seam allowance (about ⅛ in/2.5 mm).

There are some lines on your pattern pieces that you don't need to mark, including grain lines and "place on fold" lines. All pattern pieces will note a grain line (see page 10). This is just to show you in which direction to lay out your pattern piece. For pieces cut on the fold of your fabric, simply line up the edge that says "place on fold" on the fold of the fabric; no need to mark.

The project patterns all have seam allowances included, but if your sewing machine does not have a measuring guide on the throat plate, you can either mark the measurement on your machine's throat plate using the edge of a piece of tape as your guide or mark your seam allowance on the Wrong side of your fabric once you've removed the paper pattern.

Once everything is marked, you can remove your paper pattern pieces and number your fabric pieces on the Wrong side (using your marking tool) to remember which is which.

Figure 7

 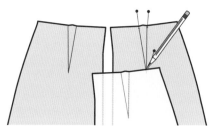

Pin mark end points   Lift pattern away   Mark line along pin points on both sides

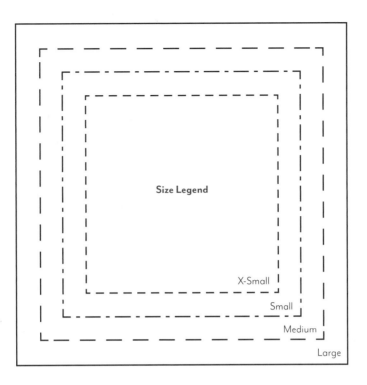

Size Legend

X-Small

Small

Medium

Large

Pattern Legend

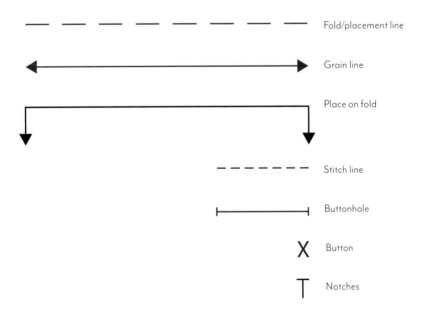

Fold/placement line

Grain line

Place on fold

Stitch line

Buttonhole

X   Button

T   Notches

THE BASICS

BEYOND THE BASICS

ADDING SHAPE

For beginning and experienced sewers alike, here's a quick overview of some beloved sewing tricks that will take your creations to the next level: darts, pleats, and gathers.

DARTS

Darts, which appear on patterns as triangular markings, give your garment contour and shape. Transfer the solid lines (known as dart legs) to the Wrong side of your fabric. Fold your dart in half, Right sides together, making sure the dart legs line up on both sides, and pin together along the dart legs.

Starting at the widest portion of the dart, stitch along the marking and end at the point. Don't backstitch (a reverse stitch that reinforces your stitching) at the point; instead, knot the threads at the end point (see Figure 8). Press the dart excess in the direction specified by your instructions. You can trim and finish the dart seam or leave as-is.

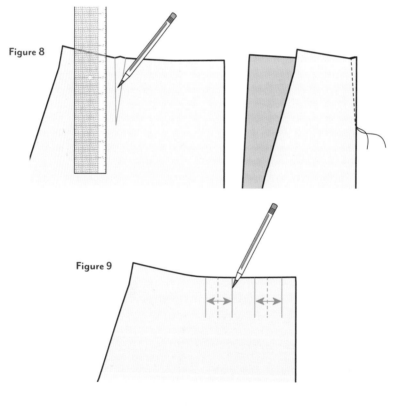

Figure 8

Figure 9

PLEATS

Similar to how you mark dart lines, mark pleat lines (which should have two solid stitch lines and one dotted fold line—see Figure 9 on page 26) on the Wrong side of your fabric. With Right sides together, fold your pleats at the dotted line (if a pleat falls on a fold, use that fold instead) and press, making sure the solid lines on both sides of the fold line up. Stitch solid lines together, press as sewn (before opening the seam), and then press the seam open (see Figure 10). Fold and press your pleat over in the direction of the arrow shown on the pattern pieces. For a box or an inverted box pleat, press the pleat centered over the sewn seam (rather than folding to the left or right).

GATHERS

Gathering, or "adding ease"—for example, below a waistband or on a sleeve cap—increases the fullness of the area, allowing for a greater range of movement and making the garment more comfortable to wear. It also contributes to the overall look of a garment. To gather fabric, set your machine stitch length to the longest setting, then stitch ¼ in/ 5 mm from the raw edge between the gathering marks on the fabric piece; don't backstitch (reversing your stitch at the beginning or end of your stitching to reinforce stitching). Repeat with another row of stitches ¼ in/5 mm from the first stitching and within the seam allowance. Gently pull both bobbin threads so that the fabric gathers evenly to the width marked on your corresponding pattern piece (see Figure 11).

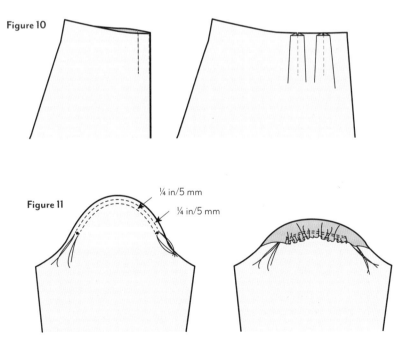

Figure 10

Figure 11

¼ in/5 mm
¼ in/5 mm

CURVES & CORNERS

As you approach a curve or corner in your sewing, the key is to proceed with caution, just as you would if you were driving around a bend or making a right-hand turn. Narrow curves and sharp corners will require you to take your foot off your machine's pedal and use the handwheel to ensure that you stay on track of your stitchline. Here are some detailed steps for sewing around necklines, armholes, and curvy pockets as well as for making mitered corners.

NECKLINES & ARMHOLES

Sewing along necklines and armholes can be tricky if you're still building your sewing skills. Again, the key is to work slowly and use as many pins as you need to keep the fabric in place.

Stay Stitching

First, stabilize the fabric by stay stitching around the curved area as follows: Set your machine to 1.5 stitch length and stitch ¼ in/5 mm from the raw edge around the entire neckline, armhole, or curved area. Return your stitch length to 2 to 2.5 before continuing.

Edgestitching

An edgestitch is sewn on the Right side of the garment, usually ⅛ in/2.5 mm to ¹⁄₁₆ in/1.5 mm from the edge of a garment hem, neckline interfacing, or around a sleeve or waistline. Topstitching is similar to edgestitching in that it is shown on the Right side but can fall anywhere the pattern calls for it. This can be decorative or function to keep seams and hems flat.

Sew Curves or Corners

When you're ready to stitch a curved piece on the project, add pins perpendicular to your stitch line about 1 in/2.5 cm apart. If your machine has a slow setting, set it at the slowest speed. Remove the extension arm on your machine. Guide the neckline or curved piece around slowly and when you approach a sharp curve (likely at a seam) or a corner (as in the square neckline in the Poppy Tank, page 85), use your handwheel instead of your foot pedal to approach it. With the needle pierced into the fabric (seam or corner point), lift your presser foot and pivot the fabric so that you stay on the seam line.

Clip Curves

Clip your curves every 1½ in/4 cm, staggering the clips by layer—meaning clip the facing first and then the self fabric (or the fabric used on the Right side) at alternate intervals. Clip close to the seam line without cutting into it to get a clean finish. For convex curves, like the ones you'll find on pockets, you want to clip triangular notches into your seam allowance. For concave curves, as seen on a neckline, you want to clip slits straight into the seam allowance (without clipping into the seam; see Figure 12).

Understitching

Facings and linings have a tendency to peek out onto the Right side of necklines and armholes. To keep them and their seams hidden, try understitching on the Wrong side. After you've sewn your seam(s), press the seam allowance toward your facing or lining. For curved areas, be sure to clip any curves first. Press your seams as sewn (before opening them up).

Press again on the Right side. Now stitch ⅛ in/2.5 mm away from the seam through the facing and both seam allowances, avoiding the Right side of the garment.

Grading Seams

To avoid bulk along a seam line from three or more layers of fabric (consisting of fabric, facing, and interfacing), grade your seams. Do this by trimming the seam allowances at different widths so that they look like stair steps. Trim the interfacing closest to the stitching because it's the heaviest. Then press seams and finish according to the individual project instructions (see Figure 13).

POCKETS

Take one look through your closet and you'll find that pockets come in many shapes, sizes, and styles. I'll show you how to make two popular styles here: the in-seam pocket, which is used on the Pixie Dress (page 42) and the Matilda Dress (page 65), and the patch pocket, which is used on the Errands Bag (page 125) and the Maker's Apron (page 143).

Figure 12

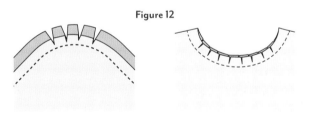

Figure 13

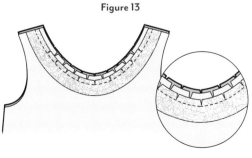

BEYOND THE BASICS

In-Seam Pockets

In-seam pockets are sewn into the seam so that they're discreetly hidden. They're often a surprise feature of a garment that you'll discover while trying it on in the dressing room, causing you to exclaim, "Oh, it has pockets, too!"

After cutting out your pocket pieces, which usually look like large mittens minus the thumb, you'll notice notches marked along the side seam of your main piece (usually around the hip). With Right sides together, align the raw edges of one pocket piece with one set of notches on your side seam; the curved part of the pocket faces inward. Pin in place and repeat by matching up the other pocket piece with the other side seam.

First, stitch the pockets along the seam from notch to notch, using the recommended seam allowance (see Figure 14). Press the seam as sewn, then open it up and press it flat, keeping the seam allowance folded toward the pocket. Edge-stitch (see page 28) along the seam, ⅛ in/2.5 mm from the seam on the pocket side to keep the pocket from peeking out to the Right side. This ensures a more professional finish. Repeat with the remaining pocket pieces.

When you reach the pocket while pinning your side seams Right sides together, pin around the outer edge of the pocket. As you stitch, slow down when you reach the first pocket attachment point. Stop, with the needle pierced into the fabric at the point, lift up your

Figure 14

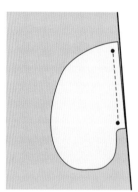
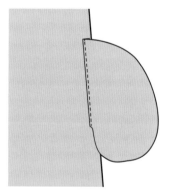

presser foot, and pivot the piece to stay within the seam allowance. Slowly turn the fabric, staying within the seam allowance, and stitch around the curved edge. Pivot again at the lower point and continue down to the bottom edge (see Figure 15).

Patch Pockets
Patch pockets are sewn onto the Right side of your garment or accessory and come in many sizes and shapes, with rounded or square corners. These pockets are both functional and decorative.

First, cut your fabric using the pocket pattern piece or the measurements noted in the cutting instructions. Then, finish the edges all around using your preferred method (see page 37). Hem the top of your pocket as the project instructions suggest. For perfectly square corners, make sure you have a perfect 90-degree angle by mitering the corners as follows: Fold down the fabric corner at your seam allowance (see Figure 16) toward the Wrong side. Fold over the straight edges so they meet in the center (see Figure 17). Hold in place; press.

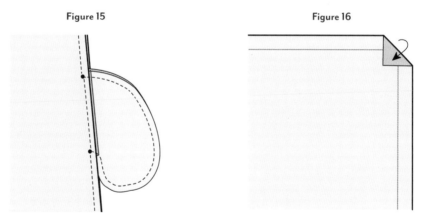

Figure 15

Figure 16

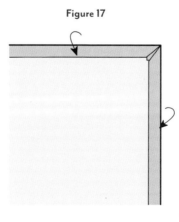

Figure 17

MAKE YOUR OWN BIAS TAPE

Bias tape, or bias binding, serves many uses in sewing, including finishing seams, substituting for facings, and adding cool embellishments. The tape stretches and bends easily, making it ideal for covering up and adorning curves and corners. You'll notice bias tape around necklines, sleeves, hems, and even quilt edges.

At some point you might find that store-bought bias tape just won't do—color selections can be limited and may not match up exactly with your fabric. If you want a more creative, customizable option, make your own bias tape—it's easy. The Picnic Tee on page 71, for example, has a cleaner finish thanks to bias tape made in the main fabric, sewn along the neckline.

To make your own (see Figure 18), simply measure with your ruler from the selvage to selvage at a 45-degree angle (this is your bias). Your ruler may have a 45-degree line on it; if not, you can fold your fabric to find it (see page 23). Mark your diagonal line and measure a parallel line 1½ in/4 cm across (or whatever width your project calls for). You may have to attach several strips together, depending on the length of tape needed (see individual project instructions). To do this, overlap two strips in an L-shape and stitch them together at a 45-degree angle. Press seams open and trim off any excess fabric that extends past the raw edges.

To make a single-fold bias tape, fold both of your lengthwise edges in toward the center of the bias tape, to the Wrong side.

To make a double-fold bias tape, follow the instructions for making a single fold first. Then fold the tape again in half lengthwise, matching the folded edges and enclosing the raw edges.

32

Figure 18

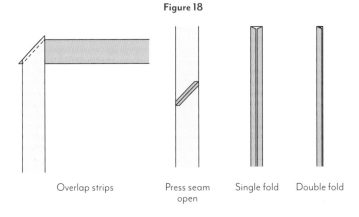

Overlap strips   Press seam open   Single fold   Double fold

CLOSURES

Adding closures like zippers, buttons, and buttonholes may seem intimidating to a beginner, but they're not so hard once you know the basic steps and practice a bit.

SEWING ZIPPERS

To apply an exposed zipper (see Figure 19), as in the Getaway Case on page 137, obtain an all-purpose zipper that has small teeth and a bottom stop. (Don't choose an invisible zipper, which does not have a bottom stop and requires a different application.) The exterior fabric of the case is fully interfaced, but if you're working with a different project, with one layer of fabric, it is smart to apply interfacing strips along the seam where the exposed zipper will be sewn for added stability.

First, lay the lining fabric Right side up, then with the zipper Right side up, align the zipper tape along one of the long edges of the lining. Then place the exterior fabric piece Wrong side down, sandwiching the zipper between the two layers. Make sure the edges align and pin the zipper in place. Put the zipper foot on your sewing machine and stitch all layers together using a ½ in/1.25 cm seam allowance. Fold both layers of fabric away from the zipper teeth and press. Edgestitch (see page 28) along the seam ⅛ in/2.5 mm from the

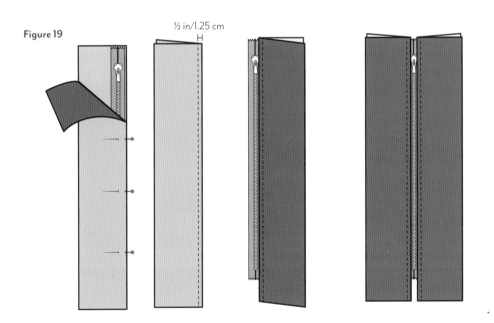

Figure 19

½ in/1.25 cm
H

seam on the fabric side of the seam. Repeat with the other fabric and lining piece on the opposite side of the zipper tape.

To install a lapped zipper, like the one used in the Lawn Party Skirt on page 116, fold each seam allowance over to the Wrong side and press ⅝ in/1.5 cm from the bottom zipper placement notch to the top of the piece (for Lawn Party, this would be the waist). Then align the pressed edge of the first fabric piece with the Right side of the zipper teeth as shown in Figure 20. You may find it is easier to have the zipper open for this step. Using a zipper foot, stitch 1/16 in/1.5 mm from the fold, avoiding the teeth but getting as close as possible.

Close the zipper and overlap the fabric so the pressed fold line on the unsewn side aligns with stitching on the opposite fabric piece and pin. The two pieces are overlapped, covering the zipper so it won't show on the finished garment. Starting at the bottom of the zipper on the second piece, slowly stitch across the bottom of the zipper, about ⅜ in/1 cm from the end. With the needle in the fabric, lift the foot, pivot, and sew a straight line ⅜ in/1 cm from the overlapped fold to the top edge (the waist). When you reach the zipper pull, keep the needle pierced in the fabric, raise the foot, and pull the zipper down past the needle to sew around it. For the Lawn Party Skirt, slip stitch (see page 39) the zipper tape to the lining and inner waistband.

Figure 20

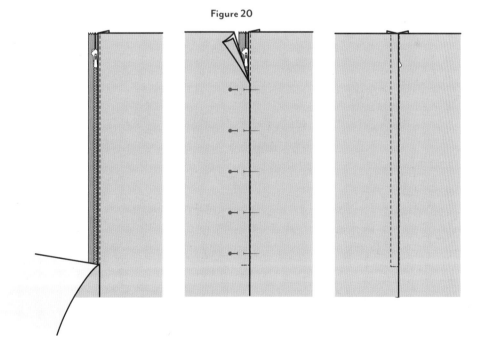

MAKING BUTTONHOLES

To make a buttonhole (see Figure 21), first transfer your buttonhole marks from the pattern pieces to the Right side of your fabric. Now find the square buttonhole stitch setting on your machine (you might also see round-end buttonhole and keyhole buttonhole settings) and set your machine to this setting or number. If you are unsure about which setting or number is your preferred buttonhole stitch, refer to your sewing machine's manual.

Locate the buttonhole foot that came with your machine. Buttonhole functions vary from machine to machine, so refer to your manual for a clear explanation for how yours works. Before you attempt to make a buttonhole on your project, do a test buttonhole on a piece of scrap fabric from your project. Note where your needle starts to stitch. (On my machine, the needle starts on the lower right side of the buttonhole.) This will help you know where to place the foot along the buttonhole markings when you proceed to your actual project.

Once complete, use your seam ripper to cut through the center of the hole. Place a pin horizontally at the top and bottom of the hole first to avoid cutting through the thread.

Finally, sew the button onto your project so that the buttonhole goes directly over it. And you're done!

Figure 21

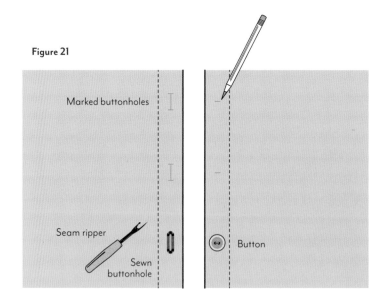

Marked buttonholes

Seam ripper

Sewn buttonhole

Button

FINISHING

Like fabric selection, the quality of your finishing can make or break a project—and a lot more is at stake at the end of a project than at the beginning. Choose from one of the following options to give your project the perfect finish.

TYPES OF SEAMS

When a project says to "finish seams" it means to clean up raw edges so they look finished and well made—and so they don't fray after some wear. First, press the seam as sewn (before opening it up), then open it and press it along the seam line. To finish, try one of these methods.

Pinking
Simply cut the raw edge of your seam allowance by half, using pinking shears for a zigzag edge. This is the easiest way to finish your seams, but it's not the prettiest. This method is good to use when you know the seam allowance will be covered by another piece (see Figure 22).

Zigzag Stitch
Stitch along the raw edges with a zigzag stitch to prevent the edges from fraying. Test your length and width settings on a piece of scrap fabric, and when you've achieved a zigzag you like, finish the seams, pressed open or closed, with it (see Figure 23).

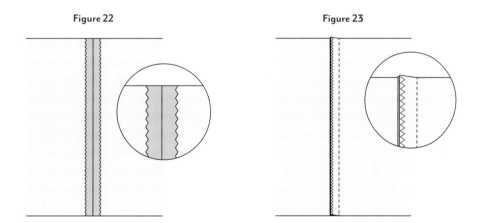

Figure 22   **Figure 23**

Edgestitch

Fold and press the raw edges ¼ in/5 mm to the Wrong side and stitch ¼ in/5 mm from the folded edge (see Figure 24).

Serger

A serger is a machine that trims and encases raw edges within the stitching. This method is easy (but means splurging on an additional machine) and delivers the most professional-looking results. You can serge each seam individually or serge them together as shown in Figure 25.

HEMMING

Never rush your hem: an uneven hem can ruin a garment—and all of your hard work—instantly. To achieve an even hem, measure, then measure again, and mark your hemline as described next before you proceed.

Blind-Stitch Hem

To prepare your hem before stitching, fold the bottom edge under, with Wrong sides together, along the hem allowance given in the project. Then, turn under the raw edge ¼ in/5 mm evenly all around. Press and pin. Using your sewing gauge or ruler, measure every 1 to 2 in/2.5 to 5 cm or so to ensure that it's even. Try on the garment to make sure you're happy with the length. For a cleaner finish, hand-stitch a blind-stitch hem to keep the stitching from showing on the Right side, as described next.

To sew a blind-stitch hem (see Figure 26, page 39), thread a handsewing needle with an arm's-length strand of thread, leaving a 6-in/15-cm tail and knotting the longer strand. Start stitching under the folded edge at the seam so the knot is hidden in the fold, and so you're only

Figure 24

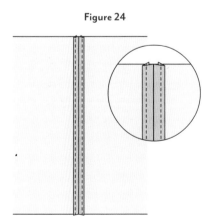

Figure 25

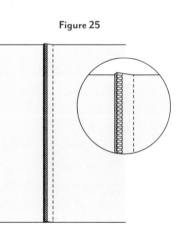

stitching through the fold, not the garment. Then pierce through to the Right side of the garment at a diagonal and make a small stitch (picking up only a few threads of the fabric) before coming back to the fold.

Stitch through the fold again and continue making small stitches through to the Right side at equal intervals, about every ½ in/1.25 cm or so. Finish off with a simple knot and hide the ends. Press when finished.

Slip Stitch

Similar to the blind-stitch hem, you can slip stitch a seam on an opening on the Right side in a way that hides the stitching. This is useful when you have to close up the opening of a pillow or quilt, like the Baby Gift Set blanket on page 156.

Press the opening's seam allowance toward the inside. Start stitching under one folded edge so the thread knot is hidden in the fold, through to the top, edging the needle closer to the inside of the fold. Every ¼ in/5 mm or so, bring the needle to the opposite piece of fabric and draw the needle under the seam's fold and up to the top in the same way. Repeat back and forth until the seam is closed. Finish off with a simple knot and hide the ends. Press when finished (see Figure 27).

Double-Fold Hem

This is a quicker hemming option, if you don't mind the stitching showing on the Right side, because you do it with the machine. Fold over and press the hem's raw edge ⅜ in/1 cm to the Wrong side, then fold the edge over again ½ in/1.25 cm and press. With your project Wrong side up, machine stitch the hem in place along the inner folded edge, making sure the bobbin thread is the thread you want to show on the Right side.

Figure 26

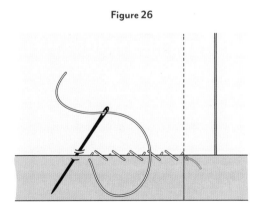

Figure 27

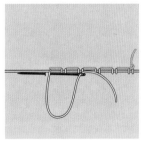

PART II: Projects

PIXIE DRESS

This classic, one-piece shift dress is the epitome of weekend ease, with a roomy, relaxed fit and go-anywhere style. The sleeveless shape is great for layering, and the practical in-seam pockets will inspire you to leave your purse at home and travel light from day to night. Get creative with fabric selection—pair two separate fabrics or use just one for sweet simplicity.

MATERIALS REQUIRED

Pattern Pieces: Pixie Dress, pieces 1–7

Notions: Coordinating thread

Fabric and Yardage: Light- to medium-weight cotton fabric (45 in/115 cm wide), cut to your desired size as appears on the yardage chart

NOTES

All seam allowances are ⅝ in/1.5 cm, unless otherwise stated.

Bottom hem allowance is 1¼ in/3 cm.

If using a directional patterned fabric (see pages 11–12), cut pattern pieces 1 and 2 in the same direction. This may require more fabric.

Optional Shortcut: Forego the pockets and simply stitch up the side seams instead.

YARDAGE CHART

	XS	S	M	L
Yoke	½ yd/0.5 m	½ yd/0.5 m	½ yd/0.5 m	½ yd/0.5 m
Dress	1⅝ yd/1.5 m	1¾ yd/1.6 m	1¾ yd/1.6 m	1¾ yd/1.6 m

CUTTING LAYOUT: PIXIE DRESS YOKE (PIECES 3 AND 4)

(45 in/115 cm wide)

CUTTING LAYOUT: PIXIE DRESS (PIECES 1–2, 5–7)

(45 in/115 cm wide)

Cutting Layout for Pattern Pieces 3–4 (Yoke)

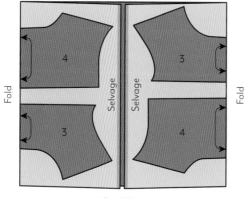

45 in/115 cm

Cutting Layout for Pattern Pieces 1–2, 5–7 (Dress)

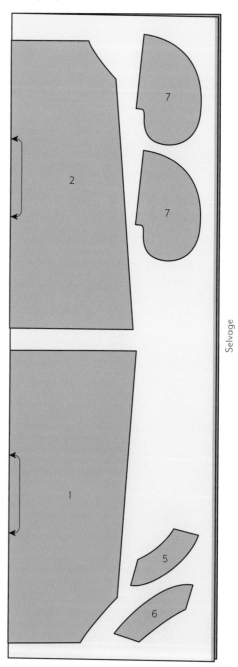

45 in/115 cm

44

PROJECT INSTRUCTIONS

PREPARATION

Download, print, and assemble the Pixie Dress pattern pieces from www .chroniclebooks.com/sundaysews. Cut out all seven pattern pieces in your desired size.

....

1. **Cut the yoke**
   a) Fold both selvages toward center of yoke fabric with Right sides together and press.
   b) Pin pattern pieces 3 (front yoke) and 4 (back yoke) to folded fabric as shown, being sure that the pieces are lined up on the fold lines as indicated, then cut them out.
   c) Pin pattern pieces 3 and 4 down a second time and cut. You will have a total of four yoke pieces.
   d) Transfer all markings to Wrong side of fabric.

2. **Cut the dress**
   a) With Right sides of dress fabric together, fold in half lengthwise, with selvages lined up. Press.
   b) Pin the remaining five pattern pieces to Wrong side of fabric, according to the Cutting Layout: Pixie Dress. Note that you will need to cut piece 7 (pocket) twice, so that you have four pocket pieces total.
   c) Cut fabric along the pattern outlines.
   d) Transfer all markings to Wrong side of fabric.

3. Sew the yoke

a) With Right sides together, align one set of the front yoke and back yoke pieces along the shoulder edge; stitch seam and press open. Repeat on second set of yoke pieces (see Figure 1).

b) Edgestitch (see page 38 and Figure 2) yoke shoulder seam on one set of the joined yoke pieces, ⅛ in/2.5 mm from seam line on both sides. This piece will be referred to as the yoke and the second set of the joined yoke pieces will be the yoke facing.

c) With Right sides together, align neckline raw edges of the yoke and yoke facing, matching the shoulder seams; pin. Stitch neckline seam (see Figure 2).

d) Clip along curves (see page 28), grade seam allowances (see page 29), and press seam open. Turn yoke Right side out and press flat along neckline seam.

e) With Right side of yoke facing up, edgestitch (see page 28) around neckline ⅛ in/2.5 mm from edge.

f) Press the bottom raw edge of the front yoke facing under ⅝ in/1.5 cm to Wrong side. Repeat on back yoke facing.

g) Fold under the yoke and yoke facing armhole raw edges ½ in/1.25 cm to Wrong side and press. Clip curves where necessary. Align the yoke and yoke facing armhole edges and edgestitch them together ⅛ in/ 2.5 mm from edge. Be sure to keep

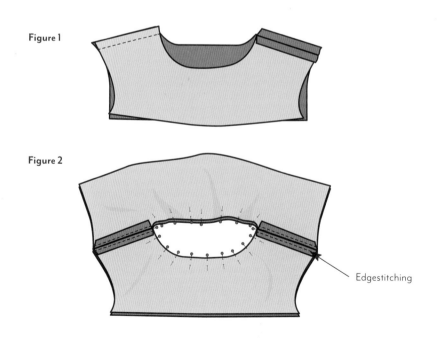

Figure 1

Figure 2

Edgestitching

the bottom edge of the yoke facing folded under to make the yoke facing ⅝ in/1.5 cm shorter than the yoke when edgestitching the armholes together. Set yoke aside.

4. Sew the dress

a) With Right sides together, align raw edges of front armhole facing to armhole of dress front; stitch facing to armhole. Repeat for second armhole. Clip curves as necessary, press seams, fold facings to Wrong side of dress, and press flat along seam; edgestitch ⅛ in/2.5 mm from edge. Finish raw curved edge of

facings (see page 37). Repeat with back facings and dress back (see Figure 3).

b) With Right sides together, align dress front top raw edge with yoke front raw edge, making sure to keep the folded front edge of the yoke facing free. Carefully stitch the dress front and yoke together, then grade and press seam allowances toward the yoke. Place yoke facing folded edge over seam allowance and blind stitch edge to the seam allowance, sewing very close to the seam line. Repeat with dress and yoke back (see Figure 4).

Figure 3

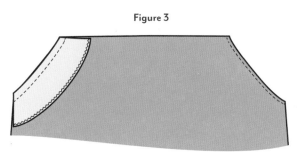

Figure 4

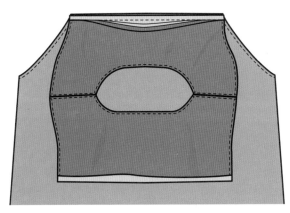
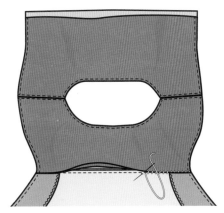

PIXIE DRESS

5. Sew the pockets

a) Align one pocket piece along side seam of dress front, with Right sides together, matching up notches on each piece. Pin pocket in place. Repeat on opposite side seam with a second pocket piece (see Figure 5).

b) Stitch pockets to dress front from notch to notch, using a ⅜-in/1-cm seam allowance. Press seam as sewn, then flip pocket over so dress and pocket are Right-side up. Press flat along seam, keeping seam allowances folded toward pocket. Edge-stitch along seam, ⅛ in/2.5 mm from the seam on pocket side. Repeat the previous two steps on dress back with remaining pocket pieces.

6. Finish the dress

a) With Right sides together, align the front and back dress pieces along side raw edges. Pin from top edge of seam (just under armhole) and around outer edge of pocket to bottom edge. Stitch side seams, pivoting at each pocket seam attachment point, and continue down to the bottom edge. Press and finish the seams (see Figure 6).

b) Fold and press bottom hem under 1¼ in/3 cm and follow the blind-stitch hem instructions (see page 38).

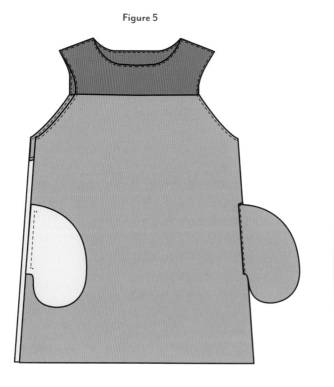

Figure 5

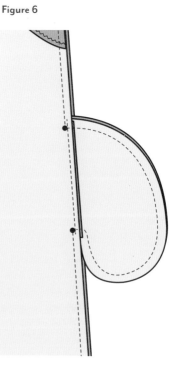

Figure 6

WEEKEND WRAP DRESS

Windy days have nothing on this wrap dress—its closed skirt, made of two simple rectangles, will keep you covered. With a flattering crossover front and a drawstring waist, it will complement your shape without confining you, making it as cute as it is comfortable. Bring the outdoors in with a sky-blue ombré cotton like this one, or use a polka-dot print for a bold, personality-packed look.

MATERIALS REQUIRED

Pattern Pieces: Weekend Wrap Dress, pieces 1–5

Notions: 2 yd/1.8 m of ribbon or cord (⅜ in/1 cm wide)

Coordinating thread

Fabric and Yardage: Light- to medium-weight cotton fabric (45 in/115 cm wide), cut to your desired size as appears on the yardage chart

NOTES

Extra yardage may be needed for self-fabric bias tape.

All seam allowances are ⅝ in/1.5 cm, unless otherwise stated.

Bottom hem allowance is 1¼ in/3 cm.

If using a directional patterned fabric (see pages 11–12), cut pattern pieces 1 and 2 in the same direction. This may require more fabric.

Optional: Want to add pockets? See page 30 for instructions to make in-seam pockets. Cut piece 7 from Pixie Dress pattern and attach the pockets to your Weekend Wrap Dress as directed before stitching side seams. For placement, measure 6 in/15 cm from waist to top of pocket.

YARDAGE CHART

XS	S	M	L
2⅝ yd/2.5 m	2¾ yd/2.6 m	2¾ yd/2.6 m	3 yd/2.8 m

CUTTING LAYOUT: WEEKEND WRAP DRESS (PIECES 1–5)

(45 in/115 cm wide)

CUTTING LAYOUT: BIAS FACINGS

(45 in/115 cm wide)

Cutting Layout for Pattern Pieces

Cutting Layout for Facings

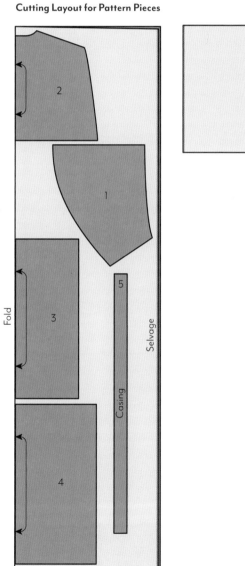

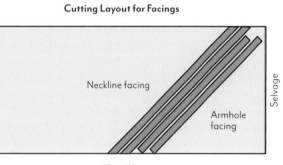

45 in/115 cm

45 in/115 cm

PROJECT INSTRUCTIONS

PREPARATION

Download, print, and assemble the Weekend Wrap Dress pattern from www.chroniclebooks.com/sundaysews. Cut out all five pattern pieces in your desired size.

1. **Cut the bodice and skirt**
    a) With Right sides of dress fabric together, fold in half with selvages lined up; press.
    b) Pin all five pattern pieces to Wrong side of fabric, according to Cutting Layout: Weekend Wrap Dress.
    c) Cut fabric along the pattern outlines.
    d) Transfer all pattern markings to Wrong side of fabric.

2. **Cut self-fabric facings**
    a) Unfold remaining dress fabric and cut bias strips to the lengths indicated in steps 2b–2c from a single layer of fabric.
    b) Neck facing: Cut 1-in/2.5-cm-wide bias strips so that when pieced together they measure at least 55 in/140 cm long.

    c) Armhole facings: Cut two 1-in/2.5-cm-wide bias strips that are at least 25 in/65 cm long.
    d) Press neck and armhole facing pieces into single-fold binding (see page 32).

3. Sew the bodice

a) With Right sides together, align front and back pieces along shoulder edges. Stitch shoulder seam (see Figure 1). Press seams open and finish seams (see page 37), then turn to Right side.

b) With Right sides together, align neckline and bias neck facing. Stitch facing to neckline with a ¼-in/5-mm seam allowance (this stitching should fall in the first crease of the bias facing). Clip seam allowances (see page 28) along the curves and press seam open.

c) Fold facing toward the Wrong side of the neckline and edgestitch (see page 28) along the inner folded edge of the facing (see Figure 2).

Figure 1

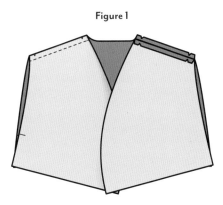

Figure 2

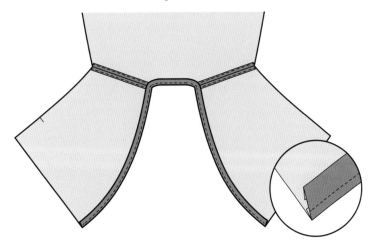

4. Sew the armholes

a) With Right sides together, align the armhole facing to the bodice between the two armhole notches. With armhole facing on top, stitch facing to armhole with a ¼-in/5-mm seam allowance (this stitching should fall in the first crease of the bias facing). Press seam open (see Figure 3).

b) Fold facing toward the Wrong side of the armhole and edgestitch along the inner folded edge of the facing. Repeat the last two steps on the opposite armhole.

5. Sew the dress

a) Overlap front pieces along the lower edge a total of 3¾ in/9.5 cm (for size XS), 4 in/10.2 cm (for size S), 4¼ in/10.8 cm (for size M), or 4½ in/11.5 cm (for size L), and baste together ⅜ in/1 cm from the raw edges (see Figure 4).

b) With Right sides together, align the lower edge of bodice front and the top of skirt front along raw edges. Stitch front bodice and skirt together and press seam toward the skirt. Repeat with back bodice and skirt pieces.

c) With Right sides together, align the side seam raw edges of the front and back pieces. Making sure the armhole edges align and the waist seams match up, stitch the side seams. Press open and finish the seams (see page 37); repeat on the opposite side seam.

Figure 3

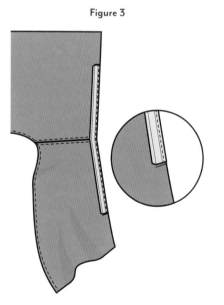

Figure 4

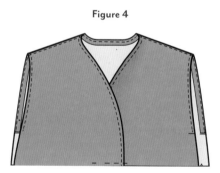

6. Add the drawstring waist

a) With Wrong sides together, fold and press each long, raw edge of casing in toward the center of the casing. Then, fold one end to the Wrong side about ½ in/1.25 cm and press.

b) Starting with this finished edge of the casing at the edge of the top piece of the two overlapped fronts, center the casing over the waist seam and pin it in place. Continue pinning casing around the entire dress, keeping it centered over the waist seam. When casing ends meet up at front overlap, trim it if necessary to ½ in/1.25 cm. Fold ½ in/1.25 cm end of casing to Wrong side and press. Edgestitch each long folded edge of the casing to the dress, leaving the short ends open for drawstring (see Figure 5).

c) Use a bodkin or safety pin to weave ribbon through casing. Hem ribbon ends to desired length so they don't fray, following the double-fold hem instructions (see page 39 and Figure 6).

7. Finish the dress

a) Fold and press bottom hem under 1¼ in/3 cm and follow the blind-stitch hem instructions (see page 38).

Figure 5   Figure 6

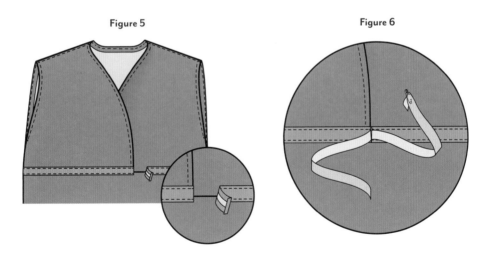

MATCHPOINT DRESS

Swing into summer with this warm-weather classic, a seersucker striped dress. Comfortable to wear to any outdoor celebration or for a simple stroll through the park, this drop-waisted dress has a modern flapper vibe while the flattering low back mirrors the Tessa Tank on page 93. With this project, you'll learn to make darts and gather a skirt waist. Try the project in the recommended seersucker or experiment with other breathable fabrics, like a Swiss dot or double-gauze cotton.

MATERIALS REQUIRED

Pattern Pieces: Matchpoint Dress, pieces 1–4

Notions: 1 package of double-fold bias tape (3 yd/2.74 m long and ¼ in/ 5 mm wide)

Coordinating thread

Fabric and Yardage: Light- to medium-weight cotton or linen fabric (45 in/115 cm wide), cut to length for your desired size as appears on the yardage chart

NOTES

All seam allowances are ⅝ in/1.5 cm, unless otherwise stated.

Bottom hem allowance is 1¼ in/3 cm.

If using a directional patterned fabric (see pages 11–12), cut pattern pieces 1 and 2 in the same direction. This may require more fabric.

YARDAGE CHART

XS	S	M	L
1½ yd/1.4 m	1⅝ yd/1.5 m	1⅝ yd/1.5 m	1¾ yd/1.6 m

CUTTING LAYOUT: MATCHPOINT DRESS (PIECES 1–4)

(45 in/115 cm wide)

Cutting Layout for Pattern Pieces

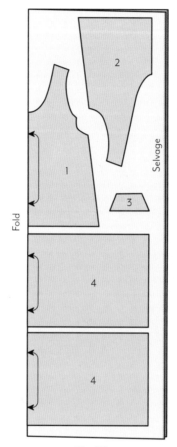

45 in/115 cm

PROJECT INSTRUCTIONS

PREPARATION

Download, print, and assemble the Matchpoint Dress pattern from www
.chroniclebooks.com/sundaysews. Cut out the four pattern pieces in your desired size.

1. **Cut the dress**
a) With Right sides together, fold fabric in half with selvages lined up; press.

b) Pin all four pattern pieces to Wrong side of fabric according to the Cutting Layout: Matchpoint Dress.
c) Cut fabric along the pattern outlines.
d) Transfer all markings to Wrong side of fabric.

2. **Sew the darts**

a) Following the instructions on page 26, with Right sides together, fold and stitch darts on the front. Press dart excess toward armholes.

3. **Sew the dress bodice**

a) Stay stitch (see page 28) around neckline and armhole edges on both the front and the back pieces, ¼ in/5 mm from edge.

b) With Right sides together, align front and back pieces along shoulder raw edges; stitch shoulder seams.

Press seams open and finish seams (see page 37 and Figure 1).

c) For back band: With Right sides of both band pieces together, align all edges; stitch along both of the longer sides using a ½-in/1.25-cm seam allowance. Turn Right side out through one short end and press flat along seams. Stitch one short end ¼ in/5 mm from edge, then finish the raw edge with either a zigzag stitch or pinking shears. Repeat on opposite end. Set band aside.

Figure 1

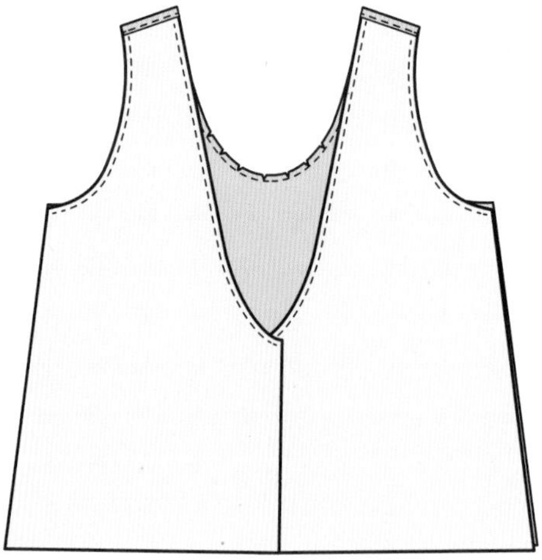

d) Starting at the center back left-hand side, pin bias tape around the neckline by inserting the raw edge of the dress fabric into tape fold (see Figure 2). Stitch bias tape in place, along inner folded edge of the tape, being sure to cover stay stitches. Repeat on raw edges of armholes.

e) Fold tape to Wrong side. Press and pin.

f) Using the back pattern piece, mark the band placement on the bias tape with pins or marker on the Wrong side. With the longer side of the band placed closest to shoulder seam, pin band in place on the Wrong side of the dress, aligning the short ends of the band with the inner edge of the bias tape. Repeat on opposite side of back.

g) Edgestitch ⅛ in/2.5 mm from the folded edge of the bias tape along the entire neckline, being sure to sew the band in place (see Figure 3).

Figure 2 **Figure 3**

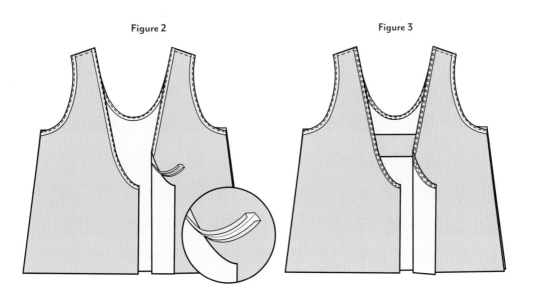

h) With Right sides together, align back pieces along center back edge and pin. Stitch center back seam. Press seam open and finish seam.

4. Sew the skirt

a) Dividing one long edge of the first skirt piece into three roughly equal sections, follow the instructions on page 27 to sew your gathering stitches along this top edge in the three divided sections; this helps ensure that the bobbin thread won't break when you pull to gather. Pull bobbin threads to gather evenly until the width of the skirt top equals the width of lower edge of Front (see Figure 4). Repeat with second skirt piece, gathering to the width of lower edge of back.

Figure 4

13–16 in/33–40.5 cm   13–16 in/33–40.5 cm   13–16 in/33–40.5 cm

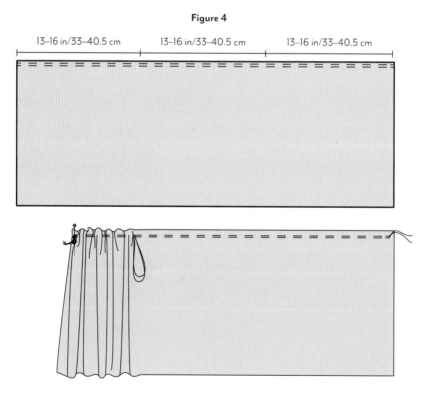

b) With Right sides together, align the lower edge of bodice front with the top edge of skirt front along raw edges (see Figure 5). Baste together ½ in/1.25 cm from raw edge, then stitch ⅝ in/1.5 cm from raw edge to secure, making sure to keep folds in gather even and flat while stitching. Press seam allowance toward body and finish seams.

c) Repeat with back bodice and back skirt.

5. Finish the dress

a) With Right sides together, align front and back pieces along side seams from armhole to bottom edge of skirt, matching waist seams. Stitch side seams. Press open and finish seams.

b) Fold and press bottom ¼ in/5 mm to Wrong side, then fold under again 1 in/2.5 cm and press. Follow the blind-stitch hem instructions (see page 38).

Figure 5

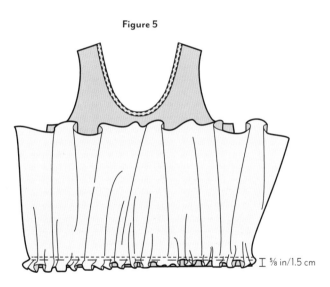

⊥ ⅝ in/1.5 cm

MATILDA DRESS

Spend your Sunday in style and comfort with this simple V-neck tunic. Convenient pockets and a neckline that pulls right over your head make this easy to sew and easy to wear, whether on its own or paired with leggings and a tee in cooler weather. Make a dressier tunic by choosing a cotton sateen (a silk blend), dress it down with a beachy sheer linen, or make an eye-catching frock with an eyelet fabric.

MATERIALS REQUIRED

Pattern Pieces: Matilda Dress, pieces 1–5

Notions: Coordinating thread

Fabric and Yardage: Light- to medium-weight cotton (45 in/115 cm wide), cut to your desired size as appears on the yardage chart

NOTES

All seam allowances are ⅝ in/1.5 cm, unless otherwise stated.

Bottom hem allowance is 1¼ in/3 cm.

Optional Shortcut: Forego the pockets and simply stitch up the side seams.

YARDAGE CHART

XS	S	M	L
2⅝ yd/2.5 m	2¾ yd/2.6 m	2¾ yd/2.6 m	2⅞ yd/2.7 m

CUTTING LAYOUT: MATILDA DRESS (PIECES 1–5)

(45 in/115 cm wide)

Cutting Layout for Pattern Pieces

45 in/115 cm

PROJECT INSTRUCTIONS

PREPARATION

Download, print, and assemble the Matilda Dress pattern pieces from www
.chroniclebooks.com/sundaysews. Cut out all five pattern pieces in your desired size.

1. **Cut the dress**
   a) With Right sides of dress fabric together, fold in half with selvages lined up; press.
   b) Pin the five pattern pieces to Wrong side of fabric, according to Cutting Layout: Matilda Dress.

   Note that you will need to cut out the pocket piece (5) twice to end up with a total of four pocket pieces.
   c) Cut fabric along the pattern outlines.
   d) Transfer all markings to Wrong side of fabric.

2. Sew the facings to the dress

a) With Right sides together, align front and back pieces along shoulder raw edges. Stitch shoulder seams; press seams open.

b) With Right sides together, align front and back facings along shoulder raw edges. Stitch shoulder seams; press seams open.

c) With Right sides together, align neckline raw edges of the dress and facing piece, matching the shoulder seams; pin. Stitch neckline together using a ⅜-in/1-cm seam allowance (see Figure 1).

d) Clip along the curves of the neckline (see page 28) and press seam open. Finish bottom raw edge (see pages 28 and 37) of the front and back facings.

e) Turn dress Right side out and fold the facing toward the Wrong side of the dress. Press flat along neckline seam.

f) Reach between the facing and dress fabric layers and grasp the two raw edges of one side of the front armhole. Pull them out together (see Figure 2).

68

Figure 1

Figure 2

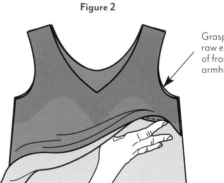

Grasp raw edges of front armhole.

g) With Right sides together, align only the front armhole raw edges of the dress and facing. Stitch along the front armhole, from side seam to the shoulder only, with a ⅜-in/1-cm seam allowance. Clip along curves and unfold so dress is Right side out.

h) Repeat f–g for the back of armhole.

i) Repeat f–h for the opposite armhole. With dress Right side out, press armhole seams flat.

3. Sew the pockets

a) With Right sides together, align one pocket piece along one front side seam, matching notches on each piece; pin pocket in place. Repeat on opposite front side seam with a second pocket piece (see Figure 3).

b) Using a ⅜-in/1-cm seam allowance, stitch pockets from notch to notch to dress front. Press seam as sewn, then flip pocket over so dress and pocket are Right side up. Press flat along seam, keeping seam allowances folded toward pocket. Edge-stitch (see page 28) along seam, ⅛ in/2.5 mm from seam on pocket side. Sew remaining pocket pieces on dress back.

4. Finish the dress

a) Open facings above the armhole seam as shown in Figure 4, page 70, so the raw edges of facing and dress form a straight line with the Wrong side showing.

b) Align front and back dress pieces along side seam raw edges, being sure to match at underarm and

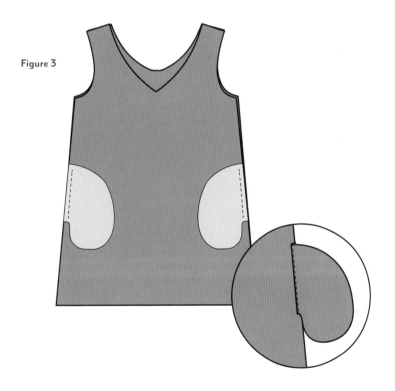

Figure 3

MATILDA DRESS

pockets; pin in place. Stitch side seams, pivoting at each pocket attachment point, and continue down to the lower edge. Press and finish the seams (see Figure 4).

c) Fold facing to inside of the dress and press flat along armhole edge. With dress Right side up, stitch facing in the side seam ditch (right over the seam line).

d) Fold and press bottom ¼ in/5 mm to Wrong side, then fold under again 1 in/2.5 cm and press. Follow the blind-stitch hem instructions (see page 38).

Figure 4

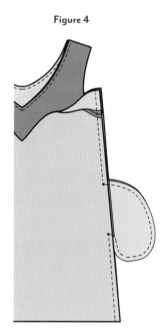

PICNIC TEE

This T-shaped top, with its simple silhouette and oversized fit, is perfect for showcasing a bold print, and plaids work well in all seasons. Pair it with cords for a fall feast or denim shorts for a summer picnic. Don't worry if things get messy—the cotton fabric is barbecue-friendly. Just throw it in the wash for easy cleanup. Cuffed sleeves and a boxy waistband round out the roomy shape, so go ahead and indulge in that extra slice of pie.

MATERIALS REQUIRED

Pattern Pieces: Picnic Tee, pieces 1–4

Notions: Covered button kit with two ½-in/1.25-cm diameter buttons

Coordinating thread

Fabric and Yardage: Light- to medium-weight cotton fabric (45 in/115 cm wide), cut to your desired size as appears on the yardage chart

NOTES

All seam allowances are ⅝ in/1.5 cm, unless otherwise stated.

If using a directional patterned fabric (see pages 11–12), cut pattern pieces 1 and 2 in the same direction. This may require more fabric.

Optional: No covered button kit? Swap the fabric-covered ones with two standard ½-in/1.25-cm diameter buttons.

YARDAGE CHART

XS	S	M	L
2 yd/1.8 m	2 yd/1.8 m	2 yd/1.8 m	2 yd/1.8 m

CUTTING LAYOUT: PICNIC TEE (PIECES 1–4)

(45 in//115 cm wide)

Cutting Layout for Pattern Pieces

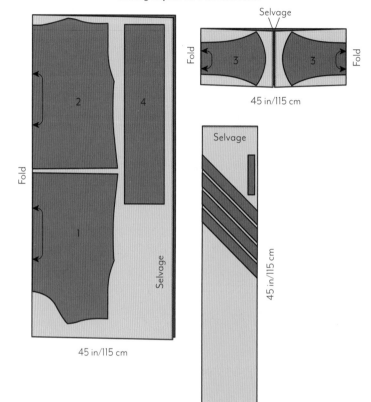

PROJECT INSTRUCTIONS

PREPARATION

Download, print, and assemble the Picnic Tee pattern pieces from www .chroniclebooks.com/sundaysews. Cut out the four pattern pieces in your desired size.

1. **Cut the sleeves**
   a) Cut a 9-in/23-cm-long strip of fabric from selvage to selvage: the piece will measure approximately 9 by 45 in/23 by 115 cm. Fold each selvage in toward center of fabric so they meet up.
   b) Pin pattern piece 3 to the Wrong side of fabric twice, according to Cutting Layout: Picnic Tee.
   c) Cut fabric along the pattern outlines.
   d) Transfer all pattern markings to Wrong side of fabric.

2. **Cut the self-fabric bias tape and button loops**
   a) Cut a 15-in/38-cm-long strip of fabric from selvage to selvage: the piece will measure approximately 15 by 45 in/38 by 115 cm.
   b) Bias tape for neck: Press the fabric flat in a single layer. Then, following the directions on page 32, cut enough 1½-in/4-cm-wide bias strips to create a double-fold strip at least 32 in/81 cm long.

   c) Button loops: Cut one 1-by-6-in/2.5-by-15-cm strip along the cross-grain and set aside (see Cutting Layout: Picnic Tee).

3. **Cut the body**
   a) With Right sides together, fold remaining fabric in half with selvages lined up; press.
   b) Pin pattern pieces 1 (front), 2 (back), and 4 (waistband) to Wrong side of fabric, according to the Cutting Layout: Picnic Tee.
   c) Cut fabric along the pattern outlines.
   d) Transfer all pattern markings to Wrong side of fabric.

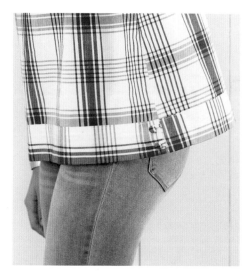

74

4. Sew the body of the tee

a) Stay stitch the neckline (see page 28) on the front and back pieces, ¼ in/5 mm from the edge.

b) With Right sides together, align front and back pieces along shoulder edges. Stitch shoulder seams (see Figure 1). Press seams open and finish seams (see page 37), then turn the top Right side out and set aside.

c) Press one short end of bias tape under ½ in/1.25 cm to the Wrong side; re-press the binding creases at the folded-under end.

d) Measure the neckline along your stay stitching and add 1 in/2.5 cm to that measurement. Cut your bias tape to that measurement, making sure not to cut off the folded-under end.

e) Pin bias tape around the raw edge of neckline, starting with the raw short end of the bias tape just overlapping the back center of the neck opening. The bias tape should fully enclose the raw edge of the neckline (see Figure 2). Overlap the raw short end of the bias tape with the turned-under end, then edgestitch ⅛ in/2.5 mm from the inside folded edge of the bias tape, being sure to catch both folded edges of the bias tape in your stitching.

5. Sew the sleeves

a) With Right sides together, align the side seam raw edges of the front and back pieces; stitch side seam. Press open and finish your seams (see page 37); repeat on the opposite side seam.

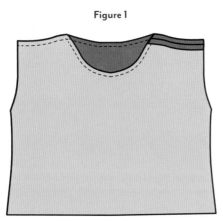

Figure 1

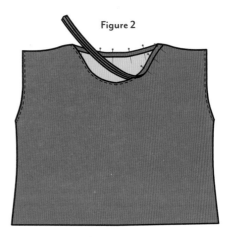

Figure 2

b) With Wrong sides together, fold sleeve pieces in half lengthwise and press (see Figure 3).

c) With Right sides together, unfold one sleeve piece and align the short ends along the raw edges. Stitch short ends together and press seam open. Then turn sleeve Right side out and refold along center crease line, aligning the raw edges. Repeat with other sleeve piece.

d) With Right sides together, align the raw edge of the sleeve with the raw edge of the armhole, so that the sleeve seam aligns with the side seam of the tee and pin. Stitch sleeve to armhole, clip curves, press seam allowance toward body, and finish the edges together (see Figure 4).

6. Sew the waistband

a) With Right sides together, place one band piece on top of the other, aligning all raw edges. Stitch bands together along one short end and press seam open.

b) With Wrong sides together, fold band in half lengthwise and press along center fold. Unfold band and press each long raw edge under to the Wrong side ⅝ in/1.5 cm, then press each of the short end raw ends under to the Wrong side ⅝ in/1.5 cm.

c) Turn garment Wrong side out. With the band's center fold open and the Right side of the band facing the Wrong side of the top, align one folded edge of the band with the raw edge of the garment; be sure to match the band join seam with one side seam of the tee (see

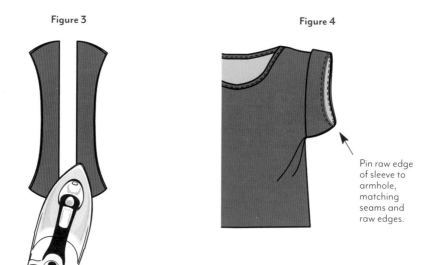

Figure 3

Figure 4

Pin raw edge of sleeve to armhole, matching seams and raw edges.

Figure 5). Stitch band to garment, and press seam allowance toward the band.

d) Turn garment Right side out, then fold the band to the Right side of the garment, enclosing the raw edge; the band's long folded edge should just cover the stitch line from the previous step. Edgestitch (see page 28) along the folded edge of the band, ⅛ in/2.5 mm from the fold.

e) Align the front band short ends and with edges turned under, edgestitch them closed, ⅛ in/2.5 mm from the folded edges; leave back band ends open.

7. Add the buttons

a) Fold the button loop piece into double-fold binding (see page 32). Edgestitch binding closed ⅛ in/2.5 mm from the folded edges. Cut in half to create two loops.

b) Make two self-covered buttons using kit. Sew buttons on Front band (see Figure 6).

c) Fold each of the loop pieces in half, then tuck raw ends of loops in between the open end of the back band. Pin them in place so they match up with the buttons, and so the loops can easily go over the buttons. Edgestitch the end of the back band closed, ⅛ in/2.5 mm from the fold, catching the loop ends in the stitching (see Figure 6).

Figure 5

Figure 6

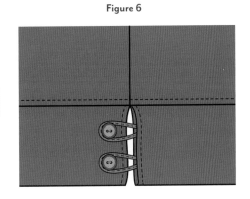

DANDELION BLOUSE

Imagine the carefree feeling of rolling down a hill of freshly cut grass. This blouse evokes that breezy vibe with its airy, gathered sleeves and wide neck—no fasteners necessary. If you choose a stripe pattern, the yoke will have horizontal stripes if you follow the cutting layout, or, for a playful touch, choose a different fabric altogether like the Pixie Dress shown on page 42.

MATERIALS REQUIRED

Pattern Pieces: Dandelion Blouse, pieces 1–6

Notions: Coordinating thread

Fabric and Yardage: Light- to medium-weight cotton fabric (45 in/115 cm wide), cut to your desired size as appears on the yardage chart

NOTES

All seam allowances are ⅝ in/1.5 cm, unless otherwise stated.

Bottom hem allowance is 1¼ in/3 cm.

Optional Shortcut: Forego the sleeves and make a simple tank by binding the raw edges like the neckline of the Picnic Tee (see page 71).

YARDAGE CHART

XS	S	M	L
2¼ yd/2 m	2¼ yd/2 m	2½ yd/2.3 m	2½ yd/2.3 m

CUTTING LAYOUT: DANDELION BLOUSE (PIECES 1–6)

(45 in/115 cm wide)

Cutting Layout for Pattern Pieces

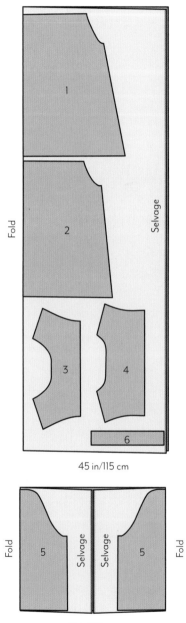

PROJECT INSTRUCTIONS

PREPARATION

Download, print, and assemble the Dandelion Blouse pattern from www
.chroniclebooks.com/sundaysews. Cut out all six pattern pieces in your desired size.

1. **Cut the blouse**

   a) With Right sides together, fold fabric in half with selvages lined up and press.

   b) Pin pattern pieces 1 (body front), 2 (body back), 3 (front yoke), 4 (back yoke), and 6 (cuff binding) to Wrong side of fabric, according to Cutting Layout: Dandelion Blouse.

   c) Cut fabric along the pattern outlines.

   d) Transfer all markings to Wrong side of fabric.

2. **Cut the sleeves**

   a) With Right sides of remaining fabric together, fold both selvages toward center of fabric and press.

   b) Pin pattern piece 5 (sleeve) to Wrong side of fabric according to Cutting Layout: Dandelion Blouse (using pattern piece twice to cut one sleeve along each fold).

   c) Cut fabric along the pattern outline.

   d) Transfer all markings to Wrong side of fabric.

DANDELION BLOUSE

3. **Sew the yoke**

a) With Right sides together, align one set of the yoke front and back pieces along shoulder raw edges. Stitch shoulder seams and press seams open. Repeat with second yoke facing pieces (see Figure 1).

b) With Right sides together, align neckline raw edges of yoke and yoke facing, matching the shoulder seams; pin. Stitch neckline together (see Figure 2).

c) Clip along curves (see page 28), grade seam allowances (see page 29), and press seam open. Turn yoke Right side out and press flat along neckline seam.

4. **Sew the blouse**

a) Gather the top edge of the front piece, between the two markings (see page 27). Pull both of the bobbin threads to gather evenly until the width of the gathered edge equals the width of the yoke front lower edge.

b) With Right sides together, align the gathered edge of the front with yoke front raw edge. Stitch pieces together, keeping the gathers even while stitching (see Figure 3). Grade seam allowance and press seam allowances toward the yoke.

c) Fold the bottom edge of the front yoke facing ⅝ in/1.5 cm to the

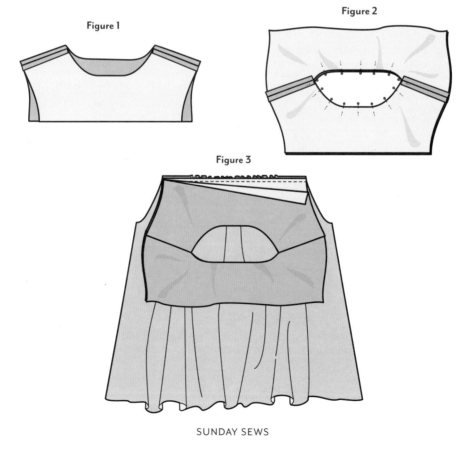

Figure 1

Figure 2

Figure 3

Wrong side; press. Place folded edge over sewn seam and blind stitch very close to the seam line.

d) To pleat back: With Wrong sides together, fold blouse back in half lengthwise. Match up solid lines and stitch along the solid lines to form the inverted box pleat. With Wrong side facing up, press pleat flat, matching fold line to seam line.

e) Baste the inverted box pleat in place along the top raw edge of the back piece, ¼ in/5 mm from the edge.

f) With Right sides together, align blouse back (pleated raw edge) with back yoke raw edge. Stitch the pleated edge and the yoke together. Grade and press seam allowances toward the yoke.

g) Fold the raw edge of the back yoke facing ⅝ in/1.5 cm to the Wrong side. Place folded edge over the seam just created and finish as for front yoke.

h) With Right sides together, align the side seams of the blouse; stitch side seams. Press seams open and finish seams (see page 37).

5. Sew the sleeves

a) Stitch gathering stitches on the sleeve cap between the two markings, then along the entire length of the bottom of the sleeve (see page 27).

b) With Right sides together, align sleeve underarm raw edges; stitch the underarm seam, being sure not to catch your gathering threads. Press seam open and finish seams.

c) With Right sides together, insert the sleeve into the armhole, matching sleeve underarm seam with blouse side seam. Pull the bobbin threads from the gathering stitches to gather the excess fullness of the sleeve and match up markings. Align the sleeve and armhole raw edges and pin (see Figure 4).

Figure 4

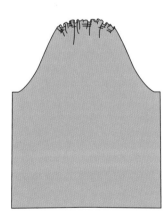

Gather fabric between notches.

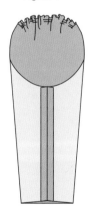

Sew underarm seam.

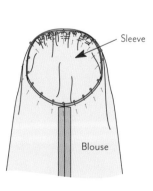

Sleeve

Blouse

Insert sleeve into armhole.

d) With Wrong side facing, start at the underarm seam and stitch sleeve in place. Press seam allowance toward sleeve and finish seams.

e) With Wrong sides together, fold one cuff piece in half, aligning the long edges, and press to create a crease. Unfold the cuff, then, with Right sides together, align the short ends and stitch to create a tube; press seam open.

f) With Right sides together, slip cuff over lower edge of sleeve, and match cuff and underarm seams. Gently pull bobbin threads and gather the lower edge of the sleeve, so that it is the same circumference as the cuff. Align raw edges and stitch together using a ⅜-in/1-cm seam allowance; press seam allowance toward cuff.

g) Fold over the raw edge of the cuff ⅜ in/1 cm to the Wrong side and press.

h) With Wrong sides together, fold cuff along center crease (from step 5e), encasing all of the seam allowances. Align cuff folded edge along seam and slip stitch in place.

i) Repeat 5a through 5h with second sleeve and cuff.

6. **Finish the blouse**

a) Fold and press bottom ¼ in/5 mm to Wrong side, then fold under again 1 in/2.5 cm and press. Follow the blind-stitch hem instructions (see page 38).

POPPY TANK

This warm-weather tank has many playful accents, including box pleats, a square neckline, ruffled sleeves, and cheerful polka dots. Free of any closures, it's easy to make and will be ready to wear by nightfall. Pair it with denim and sandals for a casual meet-up with friends or tuck it into a billowy skirt for summertime office-wear.

MATERIALS REQUIRED

Pattern Pieces: Poppy Tank, pieces 1–5

Notions: Coordinating thread

Fabric and Yardage: Light- to medium-weight cotton fabric (45 in/115 cm wide), cut to your desired size as appears on the yardage chart

NOTES

All seam allowances are ⅝ in/1.5 cm, unless otherwise stated.

Bottom hem allowance is 1¼ in/3 cm.

Optional Shortcut: Forego the sleeves and make a simple square-neck tank by binding the raw edges like the neckline of the Picnic Tee (see page 71).

YARDAGE CHART

XS	S	M	L
2¼ yd/2.1 m	2¼ yd/2.1 m	2⅜ yd/2.2 m	2⅜ yd/2.2 m

CUTTING LAYOUT: POPPY TANK (PIECES 1–5)

(45 in/115 cm wide)

Cutting Layout for Pattern Pieces

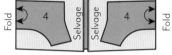

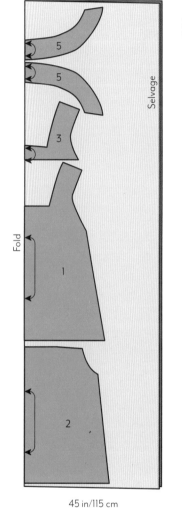

45 in/115 cm

PROJECT INSTRUCTIONS

PREPARATION

Download, print, and assemble the Poppy Tank pattern from www.chroniclebooks .com/sundaysews. Cut out all five pattern pieces in your desired size.

....

1. Cut the tank

a) With Right sides together, fold fabric in half with selvages lined up; press.

b) Pin pattern pieces 1 (front), 2 (back), 3 (front facing), and 5 (sleeve) to Wrong side of fabric, according to the Cutting Layout: Poppy Tank.

c) Cut fabric along the pattern outlines.

d) Transfer all markings to Wrong side of fabric.

2. Cut the back yoke

a) With Right sides of remaining fabric together, fold both selvages toward center of fabric and press.

b) Pin pattern piece 4 (back yoke) to Wrong side of fabric, according to Cutting Layout: Poppy Tank.

c) Cut one pattern piece on each fold to create the yoke back and yoke back facing.

d) Transfer all markings to Wrong side of fabric.

3. **Sew the tank body**

a) With Wrong sides together, fold back in half lengthwise. Match along fold line and stitch together along solid pleat lines, to form the box pleat. With Right side up, press pleat down, matching center fold line to seam line. Baste pleat in place along the top raw edge of the back, ¼ in/5 mm from the edge (see Figure 1).

b) With Right sides together, align top edge of back piece with bottom edge of yoke back; stitch back and yoke together. Press seam toward yoke and finish seams (see page 37 and Figure 2).

c) With Right sides together, align front and back pieces along shoulder raw edges. Stitch front to back and press seams open. Repeat with front and back facing pieces.

Figure 1

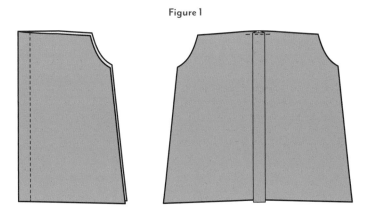

Figure 2

d) With Right sides together, align tank neckline with facing neckline, matching shoulder seams. Pin around neckline; stitch tank and facing together, pivoting at front corners. Clip along curves (see page 28) and clip diagonally at front corners. Press seams open, then turn tank Right side out and press neckline flat along seam (see Figure 3).

e) With Right side facing, edgestitch (see page 28) ⅛ in/2.5 mm from neckline edge, then edgestitch on both sides of the shoulder seams, ⅛ in/2.5 mm from the seams (see Figure 4).

4. **Sew the sleeves**

a) With Wrong sides together, fold sleeve piece in half, aligning short ends. Match fold lines and stitch at the solid pleat line to form box pleat. With Right side up, press pleat down, matching center fold line to seam line. Baste pleat in place along the top and bottom raw edges, ¼ in/5 mm from the edge (see Figure 5, page 91).

Figure 3

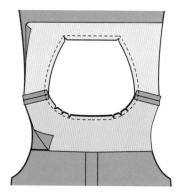

Figure 4

b) With Right sides together, align notched sleeve edge to notched armhole of tank. Pin sleeve to armhole, then stitch in place. Clip along curves and press seam open. Finish the raw edges (see page 37). Repeat with second sleeve and opposite armhole (see Figure 6).

c) With Right sides together, align side seams of tank with underarm seam of sleeve; pin along side seam, making sure to match at sleeve join. Stitch side seam and underarm together in one continuous seam. Press seam open and finish raw edges.

d) Hem sleeve edges by folding raw edge over to Wrong side ¼ in/ 5 mm and press. Then fold and press edge over again ¼ in/5 mm. Edgestitch along inner folded edge of hem.

5. Finish the tank

a) Fold and press bottom hem under ¼ in/5 mm, then fold under 1 in/ 2.5 cm, press, and follow the blindstitch hem instructions on page 38.

Figure 5

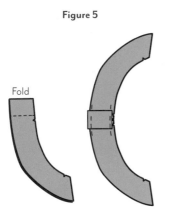

Fold

Figure 6

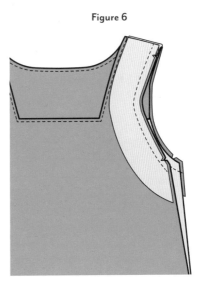

TESSA TANK

Make a memorable exit with the peekaboo low back of this simple tank. The length adds a casual comfort and looks great paired with a straight mini or skinny pant. Make the everyday piece in a lightweight fabric such as a floral cotton lawn (think classic Liberty of London fabrics) or a cool chambray and play with contrasting prints. This graphic print paired with a pop of color for the back band makes a bold mix.

MATERIALS REQUIRED

Pattern Pieces: Tessa Tank, pieces 1–3

Notions: 1 package of double-fold bias tape (¼ in/5 mm wide)

Coordinating thread

Fabric and Yardage: Light- to medium-weight cotton or linen fabric (45 in/115 cm wide), cut to your desired size as appears on the yardage chart

Band: Two scraps of coordinating or contrasting fabric

NOTES

All seam allowances are ⅝ in/1.5 cm, unless otherwise stated.

Bottom hem allowance is 1¼ in/3 cm.

If using a directional patterned fabric (see pages 11–12), cut pattern pieces 1 and 2 in the same direction. This may require more fabric.

YARDAGE CHART

XS	S	M	L
⅞ yd/1 m	⅞ yd/1 m	1 yd/1 m	1⅛ yd/1.1 m

CUTTING LAYOUT: TESSA TANK (PIECES 1–3)

(45 in/115 cm wide)

Cutting Layout for Pattern Pieces

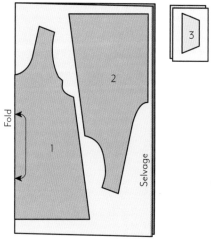

45 in/115 cm

PROJECT INSTRUCTIONS

PREPARATION

Download, print, and assemble the Tessa Tank pattern from www.chroniclebooks
.com/sundaysews. Cut out the three pattern pieces in your desired size.

....

1. **Cut the tank**

a) With Right sides of tank fabric together, fold in half with selvages lined up and press.

b) Pin pattern pieces 1 (front) and 2 (back) to Wrong side of fabric, according to the Cutting Layout: Tessa Tank.

c) Cut fabric along the pattern outlines.

d) With Right sides of band fabric together, pin pattern piece 3 (band) to Wrong side and cut along your size line.

e) Transfer all markings to Wrong side of fabric.

2. **Sew the darts**

a) Fold darts on front in half and align the dart legs, with Right sides together. Stitch darts according to instructions on page 26. Press dart excess downward.

3. **Sew the tank**

a) Stay stitch (see page 28) around neckline and armhole edges on both the front and the back pieces ¼ in/5 mm from edge. Clip seam allowance along curves (see page 28).

b) With Right sides together, align front and back pieces along shoulder raw edges; stitch shoulder seams. Press seams open and finish seams (see page 37 and Figure 1).

c) For band: With Right sides together, align all edges; stitch along both of the longer sides, using a ½ in/ 1.25 cm seam allowance. Turn Right side out through one short end and press flat along seams. Stitch one raw end together, ¼ in/5 mm from edge, then finish the edge with either a zigzag stitch or pinking shears. Repeat on opposite raw end. Set band aside.

d) Starting at the center back left-hand side, with bias tape held open, align edges of garment and tape and pin bias tape around neckline. Stitch bias tape along inner folded edge of tape, being sure to cover stay stitches. Repeat on raw edges of armholes (see Figure 2).

Figure 1

Figure 2

e) Fold taped edges to Wrong side. Press and pin.

f) Using the back pattern piece, mark the band placement on the bias tape on the Wrong side with pins or a marker. With the longer side of the band toward the shoulder seam, pin band in place, aligning the short ends of the band with the inner edge of the bias tape.

g) With bias tape folded toward the Wrong side, edgestitch ⅛ in/2.5 mm from the folded edge, along the entire neckline, being sure to secure the back band in place as you stitch (see Figure 3).

h) Finish attaching the bias tape at both armholes as for neckline.

i) With Right sides together, align back pieces along center back edge. Stitch center back pieces together; press seam open and finish seam (see page 37).

4. **Finish the tank**

a) With Right sides together, align front and back pieces along both side edges. Stitch side seams; press open and finish seams.

b) Fold and press bottom hem under ¼ in/5 mm, then fold under 1 in/2.5 cm and follow the blind-stitch hem instructions (see page 38).

Figure 3

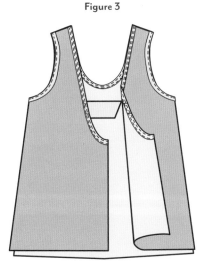

TESSA TANK

LAZY DAY SKIRT

This A-line skirt travels well from porch swings to urban parks. Blue linen—a warm-weather alternative to denim—is lightweight and breathable, and pairs beautifully with most tops. Sew the pieces together and then flex your skills in buttonhole stitching. By the day's end you'll be fastening this skirt around your favorite tee and toasting your hard work—which wasn't actually that hard—with a much-deserved glass of lemonade.

MATERIALS REQUIRED

Pattern Pieces: Lazy Day Skirt, pieces 1–5

Notions: 1 yd/1 m of fusible interfacing (20 in/50 cm wide)

Six 1-in/2.5-cm-diameter buttons

Coordinating thread

Fabric and Yardage: Light- to medium-weight linen fabric (45 in/115 cm wide), cut to your desired size as appears on the yardage chart

NOTES

All seam allowances are ⅝ in/1.5 cm, unless otherwise stated.

Bottom hem allowance is 1¼ in/3 cm.

If using a directional patterned fabric (see pages 11–12), cut pattern pieces 1 and 2 in the same direction. This may require more fabric.

Optional: For an eye-catching twist or an unexpected pop of color, use a different fabric for your waistband facing.

Optional Shortcut: To make this skirt even lazier, skip the addition of the belt loops.

YARDAGE CHART

XS	S	M	L
1¾ yd/1.6 m	1¾ yd/1.6 m	1¾ yd/1.6 m	1¾ yd/1.6 m

CUTTING LAYOUT: LAZY DAY SKIRT (PIECES 1–3 AND 5)

(45 in/115 cm wide)

CUTTING LAYOUT: INTERFACING (PIECES 3–4)

(20 in/50 cm wide)

Cutting Layout for Pattern Pieces

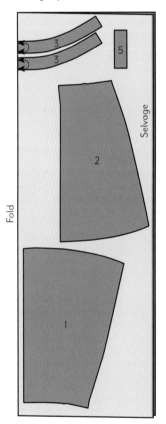

Cutting Layout for Interfacing

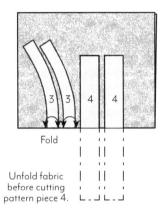

45 in/115 cm wide

PROJECT INSTRUCTIONS

PREPARATION

Turn to the back of the book to find the Lazy Day Skirt pattern. To keep this pattern intact for future use (when you might want to make the skirt in another size, for example), trace the pattern onto a clean sheet by following the tracing instructions on page 21. Then cut out all five pattern pieces in your desired size. This pattern is also available for download at www.chroniclebooks.com/sundaysews.

1. **Cut the skirt**

a) With Right sides together, fold fabric in half with selvages lined up; press.

b) Pin pattern pieces 1 (front), 2 (back), 3 (waistband), and 5 (belt loop) to Wrong side of fabric, according to the Cutting Layout: Lazy Day Skirt.

c) Cut fabric along the pattern outlines.

d) Transfer all markings to Wrong side of fabric.

2. **Cut the interfacing**

a) With Right sides together, fold interfacing in half with cut ends lined up (not selvages).

b) Pin pattern piece 3 (waistband) along fold and cut out twice, according to Cutting Layout: Interfacing. Cut interfacing along pattern outlines.

c) With remaining interfacing, unfold and open to a single layer.

d) On nonadhesive side, pin pattern piece 4 (front interfacing) twice, according to Cutting Layout: Interfacing. Cut interfacing along the pattern outlines.

e) Transfer all markings to Wrong side of interfacing.

f) Press interfacings to Wrong side of corresponding pieces; 4 (front interfacing) should line up with the markings on 1 (front).

3. **Sew the darts**

a) With Right sides together, fold darts to align the dart legs on the back skirt. Stitch darts according to the instructions on page 26. Press dart excess toward center back. Repeat on front pieces, and press dart excess toward center front.

4. **Sew the skirt**

a) With Right sides together, align back skirt pieces along center back raw edges; stitch the center back seam (see Figure 1). Press seam open and finish raw edges (see page 37).

b) With Right sides together, align the raw edges of skirt fronts and skirt back along both side edges; stitch

side seams together. Press seams open and finish raw edges (see Figure 2).

c) Fold under and press the front skirt center raw edges, ⅜ in/1 cm to Wrong side. Then fold under and press again along fold line shown on pattern piece to form the front skirt placket. Edgestitch (see page 28) along the inner folded edge of the placket on left and right front. Be sure to transfer button and buttonhole markings onto the Right side of the placket (marking button-holes on the wearer's right-hand side and buttons on wearer's left-hand side).

Figure 1

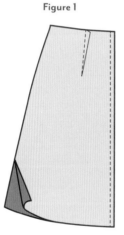

Figure 2

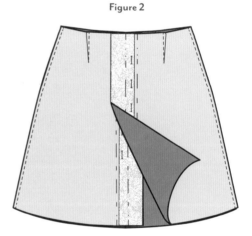

5. Sew the waistband

a) Fold and press belt loop strips as you would when making double-fold binding (see page 32). Pin aligned folded edges together and edgestitch along both lengthwise edges, ⅛ in/2.5 mm from the edge. Cut strip into three equal length pieces.

b) With Right sides together, pin belt loops along loop markings on the top of one waistband piece, lining up raw edges. Baste each belt loop in place along top edge, ¼ in/5 mm from edge (see Figure 3).

c) With Right sides together, align top raw edges of both waistband pieces, sandwiching the loops (see Figure 4). Stitch waistband together along the top edge at ⅜ in/1 cm. Press seam open, then fold waistband so Wrong sides are together, and press flat along seam. Please note that bottom of belt loops will be sewn down in step 5g.

d) Align the Right side of the waistband piece without belt loops along the Wrong side of the skirt top edge. Stitch together using a ⅜-in/1-cm seam allowance. Then, with Right sides together, stitch each of the short ends of the waistbands together, using approximately a ⅜-in/1-cm seam allowance, making sure not to catch the skirt front edge in the stitching. Clip corners at top waistband.

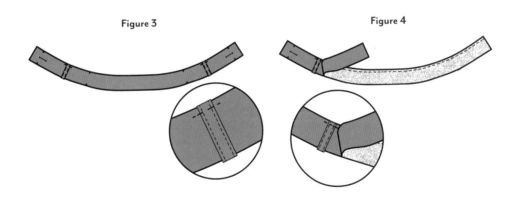

Figure 3

Figure 4

e) Fold waistband Right side out and press seam allowance toward waistband. Fold and press the long edge of the exterior waistband piece, toward Wrong side, approximately ⅜ in/1 cm, leaving the belt loops free. Pin exterior waistband folded edge to skirt, making sure to cover waistband stitching from step 5d. Edgestitch (see page 28) waistband to skirt, ⅛ in/2.5 mm from seam on waistband side.

f) With garment's Right side facing, starting at one short end, edgestitch along the three remaining sides of the waistband, ⅛ in/2.5 mm from the edge, again leaving the belt loops free.

g) Fold and press under the raw edges of belt loops by ¼ in/5 mm and edgestitch to the waistband, through all layers (see Figure 5).

6. Add the buttons

a) Machine-stitch buttonholes (see page 36) as marked on the wearer's right front skirt placket. Then, hand-stitch the buttons opposite the buttonholes on the left front placket.

7. Finish the skirt

a) Fold and press bottom hem under ¼ in/5 mm, then fold and press again at 1 in/2.5 cm and follow the blind-stitch hem instructions (see page 38).

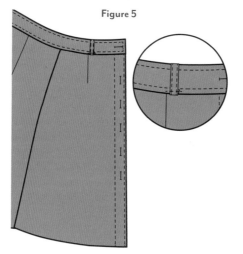

Figure 5

MONDAY SKIRT

Add a little sunshine to your workweek with this reversible pencil skirt. I paired cheerful yellow on one side to wear with a patterned blouse, and an Ikat print on the flip side to wear with a solid top. Take this skirt's endless styling opportunities one step further by adding bright buttons or by playing with day-to-night fabric pairings to go from casual to chic in an instant.

MATERIALS REQUIRED

Pattern Pieces: Monday Skirt, pieces 1–3

Notions: ½ yd/0.5 m of fusible interfacing (20 in/50 cm wide)

Four ⅞-in/2.2-cm-diameter buttons

Coordinating thread for both sides of fabric

Fabric and Yardage: Two different fabrics, (fabric A and fabric B); light- to medium-weight cotton (45 in/115 cm wide), cut to your desired size as appears on the yardage chart

NOTES

All seam allowances are ½ in/1.25 cm, unless otherwise stated.

Bottom hem allowance is 1¼ in/3 cm.

For best results, look for fabrics with the same fiber content (two same-weight cottons rather than a cotton with linen or silk) to avoid puckering and consider whether your chosen prints or colors will show through to the other side.

Before sewing the buttonholes in step 4, try on the skirt and adjust the button markings if necessary.

YARDAGE CHART

	XS	S	M	L
Fabric A	1½ yd/1.5 m	1½ yd/1.5 m	1½ yd/1.5 m	1⅝ yd/1.5 m
Fabric B	1½ yd/1.5 m	1½ yd/1.5 m	1½ yd/1.5 m	1⅝ yd/1.5 m

CUTTING LAYOUT: MONDAY SKIRT (PIECES 1–3)

(45 in/115 cm wide)

CUTTING LAYOUT: INTERFACING (PIECE 3)

(20 in/50 cm wide)

Cutting Layout for Skirt

Cutting Layout for Interfacing

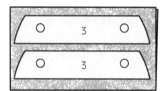

Fold

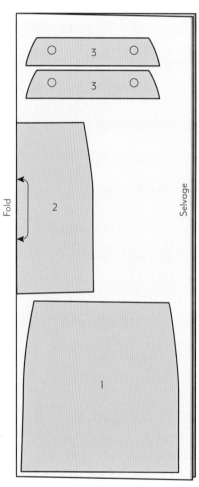

45 in/115 cm wide

PROJECT INSTRUCTIONS

PREPARATION

Download, print, and assemble the Monday Skirt pattern from www.chroniclebooks .com/sundaysews. Cut out all three pattern pieces in your desired size.

. . . .

1. **Cut the skirt**
    a) With Right sides together, fold fabric A in half with selvages lined up; press.
    b) Pin the three pattern pieces to the Wrong side according to the Cutting Layout: Monday Skirt, remembering to place and cut piece 3 for three waistband pieces.
    c) Cut fabric along the pattern outlines.
    d) Transfer all markings to Wrong side of fabric.
    e) Repeat steps 1a–1d with fabric B.

2. **Cut the interfacing**
    a) With adhesive sides together, fold interfacing in half lengthwise.
    b) Pin pattern piece 3 (waistband) according to the Cutting Layout: Interfacing. Cut out four pieces total.
    c) Transfer all markings to Wrong side of fabric.
    d) Following instructions on interface packaging, attach interfacing to Wrong side of four waistband pieces, two each of the two different fabrics.

108

3. **Sew the skirt**

a) With Right sides together of fabric A, align bottom edge of noninterfaced waistband piece with the top edge of skirt back piece (see Figure 1). Stitch together using a ⅜-in/1-cm seam allowance; press seam allowance toward waistband. Repeat with interfaced waistband pieces and the front skirt pieces.

b) Continuing with fabric A pieces, with Right sides together, align back piece with one of the front pieces along the side edge; stitch the side seam and press open. Repeat with second front piece on the opposite side of the back (see Figure 2).

c) Repeat steps 3a–3b with fabric B.

d) With Right sides together, align all edges of both joined skirts; stitch along top edge using a ⅜-in/1-cm seam allowance. Then stitch each of the front edges together using a ⅝-in/1.5-cm seam allowance.

e) Clip corners and trim excess fabric as needed around curves.

f) With Wrong side still facing out, fold bottom hem up 1¼ in/3 cm

Figure 1

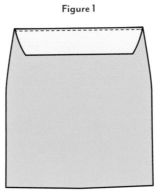

Figure 2

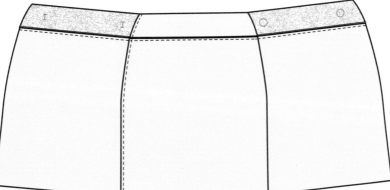

and press, making sure that both fabrics match up at lower edge. Turn skirt Right side out and press all seams and folds flat. Use a point turner or knitting needle to gently poke each corner out.

4. **Sew the buttons**
   You will be sewing two buttons on to each side of the skirt. Note that if the buttons you are using on side A and side B have similarly spaced holes, you may find it easier to sew them on simultaneously through all layers.

a) Machine-stitch buttonholes (see page 36) through all layers as marked on the waistband piece.

b) With fabric A Right side up, hand-sew two buttons on the front waistband as marked, through all layers opposite the buttonholes.

c) With fabric B Right side up, hand-sew two buttons onto front waistband piece just under the buttons on the opposite side (see Figure 3).

5. **Finish the skirt**

a) To finish the waistband, topstitch along the waistband seam (see Figure 3).

b) Sew hem in place by topstitching along bottom edge, ⅝ in/1.5 cm from the edge.

Figure 3

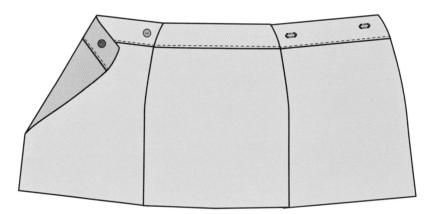

SORBET SKIRT

This polka-dot print is as fun and refreshing as eating sorbet on a hot summer day. The flattering A-line silhouette and breathable blend of cotton and linen is perfect for wearing to an outdoor gathering or a walk on the beach. The skirt's simple styling allows you to make several in a variety of prints to go with any mood or season. With its comfortable elastic waistband, the skirt slips right on and gives you enough room to go for that extra scoop.

MATERIALS REQUIRED

Pattern Pieces: Sorbet Skirt, pieces 1–2

Notions: 1 yd of elastic (¾ in/2 cm wide)

2 yd/2 m of ribbon or cording (¼ in/5 mm wide or narrower) for drawstring tie

2-by-1-in/5-by-2.5-cm strip of interfacing

Coordinating thread

Fabric and Yardage: Light- to medium-weight cotton or linen fabric (45 in/115 cm wide), cut to your desired size as appears on the yardage chart

NOTES

All seam allowances are ⅝ in/1.5 cm, unless otherwise stated.

Bottom hem allowance is 1 in/2.5 cm and casing allowance is 1¼ in/3 cm.

If using a directional patterned fabric (see pages 11–12), cut pattern pieces 1 and 2 in the same direction. This may require more fabric.

Optional: To add pockets to the skirt, refer to page 30 and follow instructions for in-seam pockets. Cut piece 7 from Pixie Dress pattern and attach the pockets to your Sorbet Skirt as directed before stitching side seams. For placement, measure 6 in/15 cm from waist to top of pocket.

YARDAGE CHART

XS	S	M	L
1½ yd/1.5 m	1⅝ yd/1.5 m	1⅝ yd/1.5 m	1⅝ yd/1.5 m

CUTTING LAYOUT: SORBET SKIRT (PIECES 1–2)

(45 in/115 cm wide)

Cutting Layout for Pattern Pieces

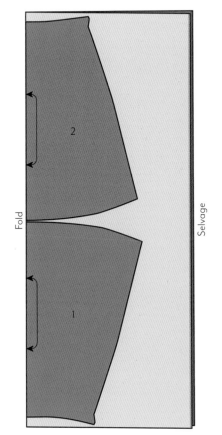

45 in/115 cm

PROJECT INSTRUCTIONS

PREPARATION

Download, print, and assemble the Sorbet Skirt pattern from www.chroniclebooks
.com/sundaysews. Cut out both pattern pieces in your desired size.

1. **Cut the skirt**

a) With Right sides together, fold fabric in half with selvages lined up; press.

b) Pin both pattern pieces to Wrong side of fabric, according to the Cutting Layout: Sorbet Skirt.

c) Cut fabric along the pattern outlines.

d) Transfer all markings to Wrong side of fabric.

2. Create buttonhole openings for ties

a) Fuse a strip of interfacing to the Wrong side of fabric at buttonhole area on the front skirt following instructions on interfacing packaging.

b) Stitch two buttonholes (see page 36) as marked (each ½ in/1.25 cm from center front) and cut the buttonhole openings.

3. Sew the skirt

a) With Right sides together, align front and back skirt pieces along side edges; stitch side seams.

b) Press seams open and finish seams (see page 37).

c) Fold over raw edge along waist ¼ in/5 mm to Wrong side and press. Fold over again 1 in/2.5 cm and press.

4. Create the waist casing

a) Stitch along lower folded edge, ⅛ in/2.5 mm from fold, leaving ⅞ in/ 2.5 cm open to thread elastic through casing.

5. Finish the skirt

a) Hem the skirt following the double-fold hem instructions (see page 39).

b) Using a bodkin or safety pin, thread elastic through one buttonhole, around waist casing, and back through original buttonhole. Try on skirt to get a comfortable fit for the elastic at your waist and cut off any excess length of elastic, making sure to leave an extra 1 in/ 2.5 cm for seaming the elastic.

c) Overlap elastic ends by 1 in/2.5 cm and stitch ends together ¼ in/5 mm from each end to secure. Tuck elastic back into the casing through the buttonhole.

d) Using a bodkin or safety pin, thread drawstring around the waist casing starting at one buttonhole and ending at the other. Knot both ends of the drawstring to prevent fraying.

LAWN PARTY SKIRT

Break out the croquet set—it's spring! This pleated mini offers the perfect mix of sporty and chic. What's best: the pleating is deceptively easy to make and will look cute in a variety of prints—from plaid to floral. Complete this project with its more intermediate lapped zipper technique, and consider yourself beyond beginner.

MATERIALS REQUIRED

Pattern Pieces: Lawn Party Skirt, pieces 1–3

Notions: 1 yd/1 m of fusible interfacing (20 in/50 cm wide)

1 all-purpose zipper, 9 in/23 cm long

1 hook-and-eye set

Coordinating thread

Fabric and Yardage: Light- to medium-weight cotton fabric (45 in/115 cm wide) and cotton lining fabric, such as a cotton batiste, cut to your desired size as appears on the yardage chart

NOTES

All seam allowances are ⅝ in/1.5 cm, unless otherwise stated.

Bottom hem allowance is 1¼ in/3 cm.

YARDAGE CHART

	XS	S	M	L
Fabric 1	1 yd/1 m	1 yd/1 m	1⅛ yd/1.1 m	1⅛ yd/1.1 m
Lining	⅞ yd/80 cm	1 yd/1 m	1 yd/1 m	1 yd/1 m

CUTTING LAYOUT: LAWN PARTY SKIRT (PIECES 1–2)

(45 in/115 cm wide)

CUTTING LAYOUT: LINING (PIECE 3)

(45 in/115 cm wide)

Cutting Layout for Pattern Pieces (Skirt)

Cutting Layout for Pattern Pieces (Lining)

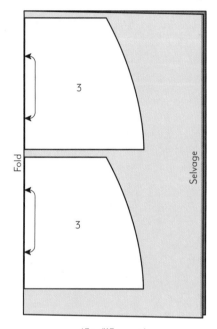

45 in/115 cm wide

45 in/115 cm wide

CUTTING LAYOUT: INTERFACING (PIECE 2)

(20 in/50 cm wide)

Cutting Layout for Interfacing

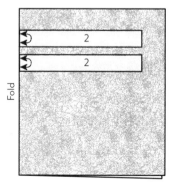

20 in/50 cm wide

PROJECT INSTRUCTIONS

PREPARATION

Download, print, and assemble the Lawn Party Skirt pattern from www .chroniclebooks.com/sundaysews. Cut out the three pattern pieces in your desired size.

1. **Cut the skirt**
   a) With Right sides together, fold fabric in half with selvages lined up; press.
   b) Pin pattern pieces 1 (front and back) and 2 (waistband) to Wrong side of fabric, according to the Cutting Layout: Lawn Party Skirt.
   c) Cut fabric along the pattern outlines.

d) Transfer all markings to Wrong side of fabric on both pieces. Please note that the top center fold of each of the skirt pieces should be marked with a dotted line just like the other pleat fold markings.

2. **Cut the lining**
   a) With Right sides together, fold fabric in half with selvages lined up; press.
   b) Pin pattern piece 3 (lining) to Wrong side of fabric, according to the Cutting Layout: Lining.
   c) Cut fabric along the pattern outline.
   d) Transfer all markings to Wrong side of fabric.

3. **Cut the interfacing**
   a) With nonadhesive sides together, fold interfacing in half lengthwise.
   b) Pin pattern piece 2 (waistband) to interfacing, according to the Cutting Layout: Interfacing.
   c) Cut interfacing along the pattern outlines.
   d) Press interfacing onto Wrong side of both waistband pieces.

4. Sew the lining

a) Working with first lining piece, fold darts as marked with Right sides facing and align the dart legs. Stitch darts according to instructions on page 26. Press dart excess toward center of lining. Repeat on second lining piece.

b) With Right sides together, align both lining pieces along side edges. Stitch the right-hand side seam from lower edge to zipper notch. Stitch the left-hand side seam from lower edge to waist.

c) Press each side seam open and finish seams (see page 37).

5. Sew the box pleats

a) On both of the skirt pieces, with Right sides facing you, fold each pleat along the dotted line, matching the solid lines and pinning them together; press along each fold to create a crease.

b) Stitch each pleat together along the matched solid lines, from top edge of skirt down 2 in/5 cm as marked (see Figure 1).

c) Flatten each pleat, aligning the seam line with the marked dotted fold line, and press. Baste the pleats in place ¼ in/5 mm from top edge (see Figure 2).

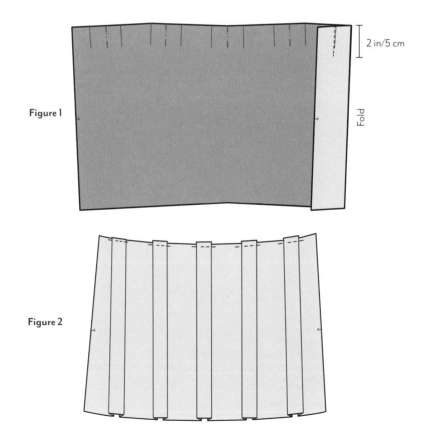

Figure 1

2 in/5 cm

Fold

Figure 2

6. **Sew the skirt**

a) With Right sides together, align the two skirt pieces along their side edges. Stitch the side seams, the right-hand seam from lower edge to waist and the left-hand seam from lower edge to zipper notch.

b) Press each side seam open and finish seams (see page 37).

c) With Right sides together, align both of the waistband pieces along all edges. Stitch the waistband pieces together along the top edge, ⅜ in/1 cm from raw edges. Press seam open, then fold waistband Right side out and press seamed edge flat (see Figure 3).

d) Turn skirt piece Right side out, then with Wrong sides together, slip the lining piece inside the skirt. Align along top edges, and match both pieces at side seams. Baste skirt and lining together ¼ in/5 mm from the top edge.

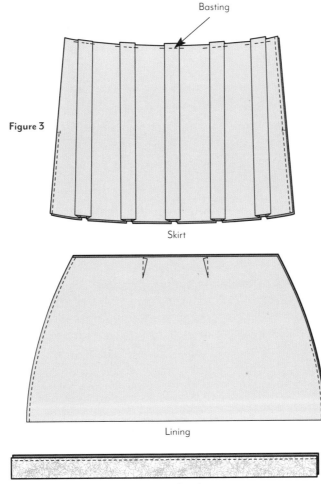

Figure 3

Basting

Skirt

Lining

Waistband

LAWN PARTY SKIRT

e) Unfold waistband piece. With Right sides together, align one waistband raw edge with skirt top edge. Stitch waistband to skirt using a ⅜-in/1-cm seam allowance. Fold waistband up away from the skirt, then press seam allowance toward waistband (see Figure 4).

f) Fold over and press the raw edge of the waistband ⅜ in/1 cm to the Wrong side. Then fold waistband in half along top edge and slip stitch the inside folded waistband edge to lining.

Figure 4

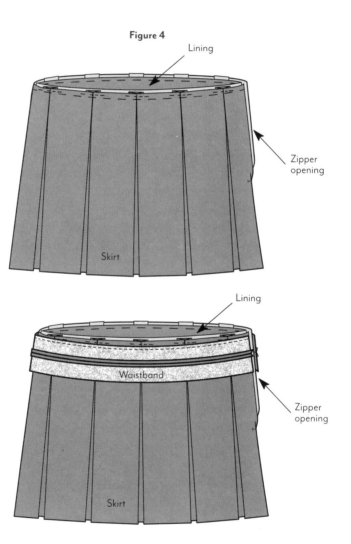

Lining

Zipper opening

Skirt

Lining

Waistband

Zipper opening

Skirt

7. **Sew the zipper and hem**

a) Insert the zipper into left-side seam opening, following the instructions for a lapped zipper on page 35.

b) Slip stitch the zipper tape to the lining and inner waistband.

c) Along the top waistband edge, hand-stitch the hook to one side of zipper tape, then hand-stitch the eye to the opposite side of the zipper tape and clasp together.

d) Fold and press the bottom hem under 1¼ in/3 cm and follow the blind-stitch hem instructions (see page 38).

e) Hem the lining following the double-fold hem instruction on page 39, taking care that the lining does not hang down below the skirt lower edge.

ERRANDS BAG

Whether you use it for your farmers' market bounty, beach towels, or a change of clothing, this everyday bag is equipped with plenty of space for your on-the-go life. Keep your phone, keys, and wallet safe with the magnetic snap on the oversized patch pocket, which nearly doubles the capacity of the bag. I chose a fabric with a very wide, bold stripe pattern for my bag, but consider natural canvas, denim, or richly toned color blocks to vary the look of this tote. Leather straps secured with rivets and a contrasting lining add visual appeal and utility to this versatile carryall.

MATERIALS REQUIRED

Pattern Pieces: Errands Bag, pieces 1–3

Notions: 2 yd/1.8 m leather strapping (1 in/2.5 cm wide)

8 rivets (⅜ in/1 cm diameter)

1 magnetic snap closure (¾ in/2 cm diameter)

Coordinating thread

Fabric and Yardage: 1 yd/1 m medium- to heavyweight cotton (54 in/135 cm wide) fabric for exterior

1 yd/1 m medium-weight cotton (45 in/115 cm wide) fabric for lining

Sizing: Bag measures 17 by 19 in/43 by 48 cm

NOTES

All seam allowances are 1 in/2.5 cm, unless otherwise stated.

Fabric used features an 8-in/20-cm-wide stripe print.

CUTTING LAYOUT: ERRANDS BAG (PIECES 1–3)

(54 in/135 cm wide)

CUTTING LAYOUT: LINING (PIECES 1 AND 3)

(45 in/115 cm wide)

Cutting Layout for Pattern Pieces

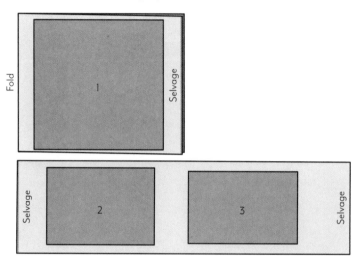

54 in/135 cm wide

Cutting Layout for Lining

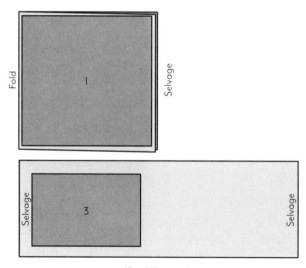

45 in/115 cm wide

PROJECT INSTRUCTIONS

PREPARATION

Download, print, and assemble the Errands Bag pattern from www.chroniclebooks
.com/sundaysews. Cut out all three pattern pieces.

1.   Cut the bag exterior

a)   With Right sides together, fold fabric in half with selvages lined up; press.

b)   Pin pattern piece 1 (front and back) on Wrong side of fabric, according to Cutting Layout: Errands Bag.

c)   Cut fabric along the pattern outlines.

d)   Unfold remaining fabric (single layer) and pin pattern pieces 2 (pocket) and 3 (pocket flap), according to Cutting Layout: Errands Bag.

e)   Cut fabric along the pattern outlines.

f)   Transfer all markings to Wrong side of fabric.

2. Cut the lining

a)   Repeat steps 1a–1c with lining fabric.

b)   Unfold remaining fabric (single layer) and pin pattern piece 3 (pocket flap), according to Cutting Layout: Lining.

c)   Cut fabric along the pattern outlines.

ERRANDS BAG

3. **Sew the pocket**

a) Double-fold hem (see page 39) the pocket sides to the Wrong side and press.

b) Double-fold hem (see page 39) the top edge of the pocket.

c) Following the manufacturer's instructions, center and install magnetic snap bottom as marked on pocket piece.

d) Center and align bottom edge of pocket with bottom edge of front with both Right sides facing up.

e) Topstitch (see page 28) pocket sides to piece, ¼ in/5 mm from double-folded edges.

f) With Right sides together, align all edges of the pocket flap with flap lining; starting at one corner stitch flap pieces together along one short side, along one long side, and up the opposite short side, leaving one long side open. Trim excess fabric from sewn corners, then turn flap Right side out. With a turning tool, gently push out the corners and press all seams flat.

g) Fold and press the open raw edge of the pocket flap and pocket flap lining 1 in/2.5 cm to Wrong side and press.

h) Topstitch along the three sewn edges of the pocket flap ¼ in/ 5 mm from edge.

i) Working through the flap's top opening and using manufacturer's directions, center and install magnetic snap top, ½ in/1.25 cm from lower edge seam, through the lining fabric only. Make sure that the snap is facing out on Right side of lining fabric, to align with snap piece on pocket.

j) With the snap shut, center and align the pocket flap about 4 in/ 10 cm above pocket, pin in place, and topstitch ¼ in/5 mm from top folded edge (see Figure 1).

4. **Sew the lining**

a) With Right sides together, align front and back pieces of lining along all edges; stitch together along both sides and lower edge.

b) Cut off excess seam allowance at the two lower corners.

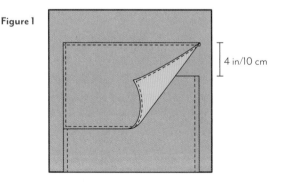

Figure 1

4 in/10 cm

c) Fold over and press the top edge of the lining 1 in/2.5 cm to Wrong side and stitch ½ in/1.25 cm from fold. Set aside.

5. Sew the bag

a) With Right sides together, align front and back pieces of bag along all edges, then stitch together along both sides and lower edge.

b) Cut off excess fabric at the two lower corners. Turn bag Right side out, use point turner to push out corners, and press all seams flat.

c) Fold top of bag over 1 in/2.5 cm to Wrong side and press. Then stitch ½ in/1.25 cm from fold.

d) Insert lining into bag, with Wrong sides together, and align both top edges with side seams matching. Fold both top edges together 1 in/ 2.5 cm to Wrong side. Press and pin.

6. Cut and attach the straps

a) Cut two 33-in/84-cm lengths from leather strapping.

b) Measure and mark 4½ in/11.5 cm toward center from each side seam, along top edge of bag on front and back using pins or water-soluble marker.

c) With Right sides together, align the end of one strap with top edge of exterior bag, placing the strap just inside mark made in step 6b. Pin in place. Repeat with the opposite end of the strap (see Figure 2). Do the same thing with the second strap on the other side of the bag.

d) Stitch around top folded edge of bag, ¼ in/5 mm from fold, catching bag strap ends in this stitching. Then stitch-in-the-ditch (or, into the seam), through all layers, along side seams 1 in/2.5 cm down from top edge.

e) With Right sides together, and the strap flat along bag, stitch across strap 1½ in/4 cm from top edge. Repeat at each strap join (see Figure 2).

f) Fold straps over at the bottom stitching, so that Right side of strap is now facing out.

g) Using your awl and a hammer, center and install two rivets (see page 18) on each strap end, making sure that the more decorative side of the rivet is on the Right side. Rivets should go all the way through to the bag interior.

129

Figure 2

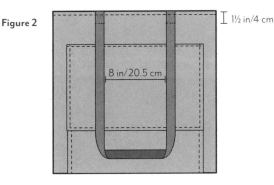

8 in/20.5 cm

I 1½ in/4 cm

ERRANDS BAG

SPRING CLEAN TOTE

Hide towels, toys, magazines, and more inside this classic yet modern storage container. Plastic canvas keeps the bottom flat while the collapsible body makes it simple to stow away when you've got company. A wide-stripe home décor cotton—heavier weight than fashion fabrics—adds stability while a cotton poplin lining creates interest with an unexpected print. Make Sunday cleaning less of a chore by keeping this in kids' rooms, bathrooms, or any room in need of a little extra storage space. Or you can eliminate the plastic canvas lining and use this oversized tote as a weekend travel bag.

....

MATERIALS REQUIRED

Pattern Pieces: Spring Clean Tote, pieces 1–3

Notions: ¼ yd /0.25 m of midweight interfacing

16-by-11-in/40.5-by-28-cm piece of plastic canvas or cardboard

1 yd/1 m of ribbon or webbing (2 in/ 5 cm wide)

Coordinating thread

Fabric and Yardage: 1½ yd/1.5 m medium- to heavyweight cotton (54 in/135 cm wide) for exterior fabric

1½ yd/1.5 m medium-weight cotton (45 in/115 cm wide) for lining fabric

Sizing: Tote measures 14 by 16 by 11 in/ 35.5 by 40.5 by 28 cm

NOTES

All seam allowances are 1 in/2.5 cm, unless otherwise stated.

Optional: Sew a patch pocket on the side for extra storage. See page 31 for instructions on sewing patch pockets.

This pattern is cut on the cross-grain of the fabric. Depending on the fabric you choose, you may want to change the grain line on the pattern as you lay out your pieces; for some fabrics this may require extra yardage.

CUTTING LAYOUT: SPRING CLEAN TOTE (PIECES 1–3)

(54 in/135 cm wide)

Cutting Layout for Pattern Pieces

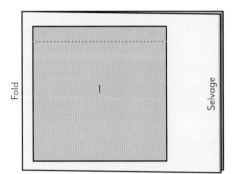

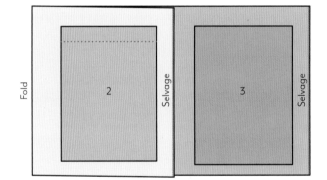

54 in/135 cm wide

CUTTING LAYOUT: LINING (PIECES 1–3)

(45 in/115 cm wide)

CUTTING LAYOUT: INTERFACING

(20 in/50 cm wide)

Cutting Layout for Lining

Cutting Layout for Interfacing

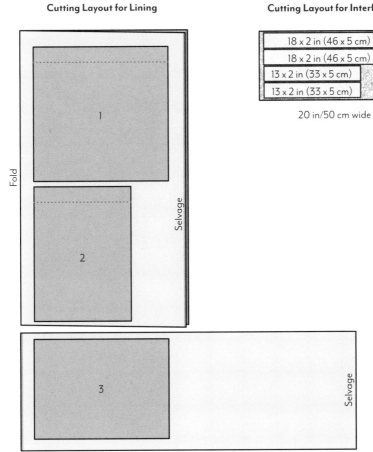

18 x 2 in (46 x 5 cm)

18 x 2 in (46 x 5 cm)

13 x 2 in (33 x 5 cm)

13 x 2 in (33 x 5 cm)

20 in/50 cm wide

Fold

Selvage

Selvage

1

2

3

45 in/115 cm wide

SPRING CLEAN TOTE

PROJECT INSTRUCTIONS

PREPARATION

Download, print, and assemble the Spring Clean Tote pattern from www
.chroniclebooks.com/sundaysews. Cut out all three pattern pieces.

1. **Cut the tote exterior**
   a) With Right sides together, fold fabric in half with selvages lined up; press.
   b) Pin the three pattern pieces to Wrong side of fabric, according to Cutting Layout: Spring Clean Tote. *Note:* Only one piece is cut from 3 (bottom).
   c) Cut fabric along the pattern outlines.
   d) Mark a 1-in/2.5-cm seam allowance at each lower corner of the front, back, and sides.

2. **Cut the lining**
   a) Repeat steps 1a–1d according to Cutting Layout: Lining. *Note:* Only one piece is cut from 3 (bottom) for lining.

3. **Cut the interfacing**
   a) Lay interfacing out in a single layer.
   b) Mark and cut two strips, each 18 by 2 in/46 by 5 cm, and two strips each 13 by 2 in/33 by 5 cm according to the Cutting Layout: Interfacing.
   c) With your iron, or according to manufacturer's instructions, attach the longer strips of interfacing to the Wrong side of the top edge of the exterior front and back pieces; attach the shorter strips to the Wrong side of the top edge of both exterior side pieces.

4. **Sew the tote exterior**

a) With Right sides together, align one front/back piece with one side piece along the side that measures 17½ in/44.5 cm. Stitch pieces together, stopping at the bottom seam allowance marks (1 in/2.5 cm from bottom edge). Repeat this step on each edge that measures 17½ in/44.5 cm, until you have joined them all together, creating a bottomless box. Press seams open (see Figure 1).

b) With Right sides together, align the edges of the bottom piece with the corresponding bottom edges of the box assembled in 4a; pin. Stitch the bottom in place around all sides; clip corners and press all seams open. Turn the tote Right side out and use a point turner to poke out corners from Wrong side.

5. **Sew the lining**

a) Repeat steps 4a–4b with lining fabric, but don't turn the lining piece Right side out (see Figure 2).

Figure 1

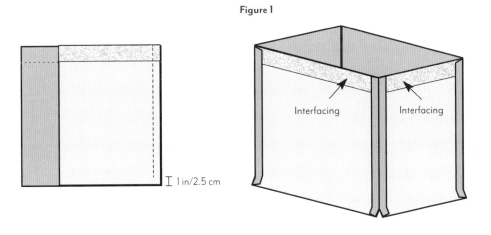

 1 in/2.5 cm

Interfacing   Interfacing

Figure 2

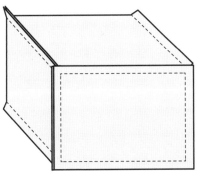

6. **Insert the plastic canvas**

a) Place the plastic canvas piece inside the tote exterior and orient along the bottom, trimming if necessary for a good fit. Slip the lining inside the tote exterior, with Wrong sides together, and match up all the seams.

b) With Wrong sides together, align the exterior and lining pieces along the top raw edge. Baste the top edge of both pieces together and trim any uneven edges; the top edges are now treated as one.

c) Double-fold hem the top of the tote as follows: Fold and press the top edge over ½ in/1.25 cm toward inside of the tote. Fold and press the top edge over again, 2 in/5 cm toward the inside of the tote and pin in place. Stitch around the top edge along the lower fold of the hem.

d) Hand-tack (see page 14) the corners of the lining to the corners of the tote exterior to secure the plastic canvas in place.

7. **Sew the straps**

a) Cut your webbing or ribbon in half.

b) Fold the short raw edges over ½ in/1.25 cm to Wrong side and press, if appropriate for your fabric.

c) Mark the wide sides of the bag 3 in/7.5 cm from the edge on each side. Using these marks as a guide, place straps near the top edge with the folded edge of the strap even with the hem stitching on the tote (step 6c) as shown in Figure 3; pin in place.

d) Stitch straps to bag with a 1½-in/4-cm square and add a diagonal cross (X) to the center of each square (see Figure 4).

Figure 3

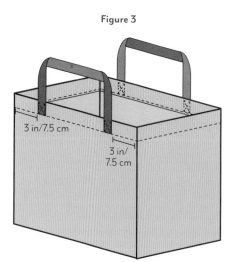

3 in/7.5 cm

3 in/7.5 cm

Figure 4

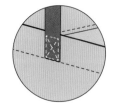

GETAWAY CASE

Skipping town for the weekend? Whether you're heading to the mountains or the beach, this spacious case can carry your getaway essentials in style. An exposed zipper closure keeps your personals from spilling into your suitcase and a hanging loop makes it convenient to grab and go. The case is lined and washable, too, so be sure to prewash your fabrics before sewing to keep this case looking great wash after wash. Choose a medium- to heavyweight cotton and gift it to the jet-setter or woodsy wanderer in your life.

MATERIALS REQUIRED

Pattern Pieces: Getaway Case, pieces 1–3

Notions: $\frac{5}{8}$ yd/0.6 m fusible interfacing (20 in/50 cm wide)

15 in/38 cm standard zipper

1 package of bias tape piping ($\frac{1}{2}$ in/ 1.25 cm wide)

1 yd/1 m of twill tape (1 in/2.5 cm wide)

Coordinating thread

Fabric and Yardage: $\frac{1}{2}$ yd/0.5 m medium- to heavyweight cotton (45 in/115 cm wide) fabric for exterior

$\frac{1}{2}$ yd/0.5 m light- to medium-weight cotton (45 in/115 cm wide) fabric for lining

Sizing: Case measures approximately 5 by 10 by 4 in/12 by 25 by 10 cm

NOTES

All seam allowances are $\frac{3}{8}$ in/1 cm, unless otherwise stated.

Install a zipper foot on your machine before starting.

CUTTING LAYOUT: GETAWAY CASE AND LINING (PIECES 1–3)

(45 in/115 cm wide)

CUTTING LAYOUT: INTERFACING (PIECES 1–3)

(20 in/50 cm wide)

Cutting Layout for Case and Lining

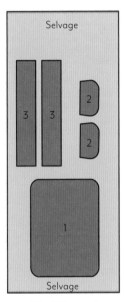

45 in/115 cm wide

Cutting Layout for Interfacing

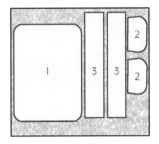

20 in/50 cm wide

PROJECT INSTRUCTIONS

PREPARATION

Download, print, and assemble the Getaway Case pattern from www.chroniclebooks.com/sundaysews. Cut out all three pattern pieces.

....

1. **Cut the bag exterior**
   a) Open fabric to a single layer and press.
   b) Pin the three pattern pieces to the fabric, according to the Cutting Layout: Getaway Case and Lining.
   c) Cut fabric along the pattern outlines.
   d) Transfer all notch markings to Wrong side of fabric for all pieces.

2. **Cut the lining**
   a) Repeat steps 1a–1d with lining fabric.

3. **Cut the interfacing and tape**
   a) Repeat steps 1a–1d with interfacing, according to Cutting Layout: Interfacing.
   b) Fuse interfacing to Wrong side of exterior fabric pieces.
   c) Clip notches ¼ in/5 mm into the seam.
   d) Cut a 6-in/15-cm piece from the twill tape for the hanging loop. Set remaining tape aside for later.

4. Sew the piping

a) For each piece of the case, with Wrong sides together and exterior fabric facing up, align all edges of the exterior and lining. Pin piping around the entire perimeter of the body piece through all layers, aligning the raw edges of the piping with the body's raw edges.

b) Attach the zipper foot to your sewing machine and baste piping to the body pieces, basting as close to the cording of the piping as possible. Where the piping begins and ends, cross the ends and stitch across this point. Clip off excess piping (see Figure 1).

5. Sew the zipper and sides

a) Insert zipper into the exterior and lining zipper placket pieces, following the exposed zipper instructions on page 33. You will want the zipper head to be about ¾ in/2 cm from one of the short ends of the placket (see Figures 2 and 3). Be sure to orient the zipper so the exterior fabric will face out when the zipper is installed.

b) Align raw edge of a strip of piping and both short ends of the hanging loop with one short end of the zipper placket (exterior fabric facing up), centering the hanging loop over the zipper.

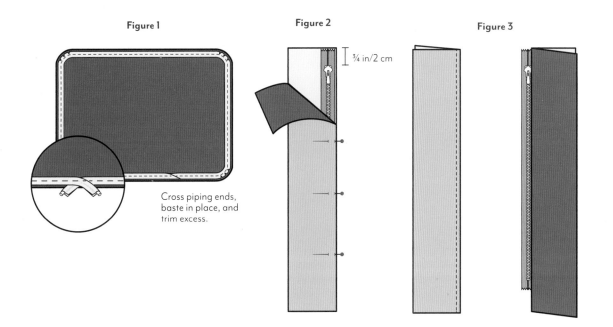

Figure 1

Cross piping ends, baste in place, and trim excess.

Figure 2

¾ in/2 cm

Figure 3

c) Pin piping and hanging loop in place and baste all layers together ⅜ in/1 cm from edge. Repeat on the opposite short end of zipper placket, but with piping only.

d) Place one lining side piece Right side up, align zipper placket, Right side up, then place on exterior side piece, Right side down on top, sandwiching the placket between the two side pieces. With edges aligned, stitch all layers together; fold side pieces away from zipper placket and press. Repeat with other end of zipper placket and remaining side pieces.

6. **Sew the bag**

a) With Right sides together, matching up all notches, carefully align the raw edges of the joined zipper placket and sides to the case body; pin (see Figure 4).

b) Open zipper (to be able to turn case Right side out once sewn). Stitch around the entire perimeter of the bag. Trim all seam allowances to ¼ in/5 mm and notch along all curves.

c) Fold and press the remaining twill tape in half lengthwise. With Wrong side of bag still facing, wrap the tape around the raw edges of all seam allowances and pin in place, (the edges of the tape should just barely cover the bag stitching). Fold over one of the short raw ends and overlap it with the other raw end (see Figure 5).

d) Stitch tape in place, ⅜ in/1 cm from folded edge, making sure to catch both edges of tape in your stitching.

e) Turn case Right side out.

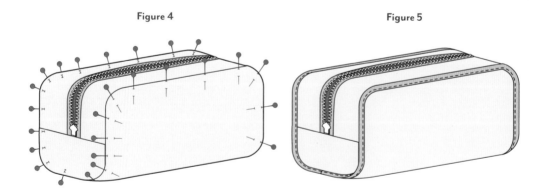

Figure 4   Figure 5

MAKER'S APRON

This one-size-fits-all apron is the perfect way to keep clean, whether you're a maker, a baker, or just someone prone to spills. To change its size, simply slide the adjustable straps through the casing around the armholes and—voilà!—any cook in your kitchen can wear it (for a kid's version, see page 163). Two patch pockets allow you to stash your phone or your recipe while you work, too. Get creative with prints: go for classic checks or bright solids, or get fancy with floral prints to suit your brunch style. Pass the pancakes, please!

MATERIALS REQUIRED

Pattern Pieces: Maker's Apron, pieces 1–3

Notions: 3¼ yd/3 m of ribbon or twill tape (1 in/2.5 cm wide)

1 yd/1 m of Wonder Tape (optional)

Coordinating thread

Fabric and Yardage: 1 yd/1 m medium-to heavyweight cotton or linen fabric (45 in/115 cm wide)

Sizing: One size fits all

NOTES

All seam allowances and bottom hem are 1 in/2.5 cm, unless otherwise stated.

Optional Shortcut: Skip the patch pocket and get cooking.

CUTTING LAYOUT: MAKER'S APRON (PIECES 1–3)

(45 in/115 cm wide)

Cutting Layout for Pattern Pieces

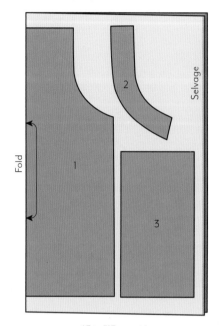

45 in/115 cm wide

PROJECT INSTRUCTIONS

PREPARATION

Download, print, and assemble the Maker's Apron pattern from www.chroniclebooks .com/sundaysews. Cut out all three pattern pieces.

1. **Cut the apron**
   a) With Right sides together, fold fabric in half with selvages lined up; press.
   b) Pin all pattern pieces to Wrong side of fabric according to Cutting Layout: Maker's Apron.

   c) Cut fabric along the pattern outlines; cut pocket on one layer of fabric only.
   d) Transfer all markings to Wrong side of fabric.

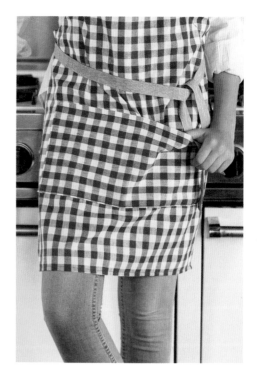

SEWING INSTRUCTIONS

2. **Sew the apron and facings**

a) Hem top, side, and bottom edges of apron, following the double-fold hem instructions on page 39. Do not hem along curved arm openings.

b) Double-fold hem each short edge of the two facing pieces.

c) With Right sides together, align apron and facing pieces along armhole curves and pin; stitch facings to apron armhole curves using a ½-in/1.25-cm seam allowance (see Figure 1). Clip the seam allowance along curves and press seam open. Then fold and press the facings to the Wrong side of the apron.

d) To finish the raw edges of the facings, fold over ½ in/1.25 cm to the Wrong side and press. Stitch the facing to the apron, ⅛ in/2.5 mm from the inner folded edge of the facing. This creates the armhole casings for the ties.

Figure 1

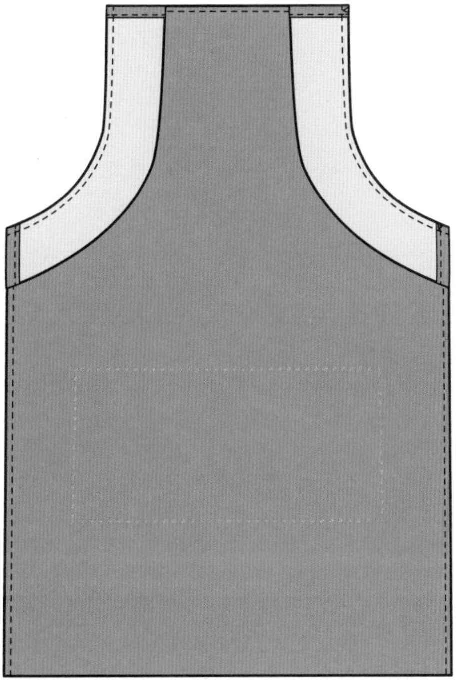

3. **Sew the pocket**

a) Double-fold hem (see page 39) one long edge of the pocket piece. This hemmed edge is now the top of the pocket. Be sure to stitch along this hem.

b) Double-fold hem (see page 39) the seam allowance of sides and bottom pocket to the Wrong side and press.

c) Use Wonder Tape or pins to align the pocket sides and bottom to the center front of apron at pocket markings.

d) Starting at one top corner, stitch around the three sides of the pocket, ⅛ in/2.5 mm from the folded edge, leaving the top open.

e) Divide the pocket by stitching up the center of the pocket to create two pockets.

4. **Add the tie**

a) Double-fold hem the raw edges of the ribbon or tape.

b) Use a bodkin or safety pin to thread ribbon/tape through armhole casings. Start threading the ribbon/tape at the bottom of one side opening, then out the top opening and back down the top opening of the opposite armhole casing. You will want to leave a long loop of ribbon/tape at the top for your head to slip through.

c) Wear and serve.

BIRDIE DRESS

Nothing says spring like a sundress with butterfly sleeves and bright floral patterns. Japanese Nani Iro double-gauze cotton fabric feels light and delicate in a nature-inspired print, but the options here are endless: try a colorful gingham or any quilting cotton fabric to match your tot's budding personality. The curvy sleeve achieves a sweet ruffle with a simple gathering technique and a button closure adds a special detail while keeping it simple for mom to put over squirmy little ones.

MATERIALS REQUIRED

Pattern Pieces: Birdie Dress, pieces 1–3

Notions: One button (½ in/1.25 cm in diameter) for back closure

Coordinating thread

Fabric and Yardage: Light- to medium-weight cotton or linen fabric (45 in/115 cm wide), cut to your desired size (see Birdie Dress Size Chart) as appears on the yardage chart

NOTES

All seam allowances are ⅝ in/1.5 cm, unless otherwise stated.

Bottom hem allowance is 1¼ in/3 cm.

BIRDIE DRESS SIZE CHART

	Chest	Waist	Hip
2T	21 in/53 cm	20 in/51 cm	22 in/56 cm
3T	22 in/56 cm	20½ in/52 cm	23 in/58 cm
4T	23 in/58 cm	21 in/53 cm	24 in/61 cm

YARDAGE CHART

2T	3T	4T
⅞ yd/0.8m	1 yd/1 m	1¼ yd/1.2 m

CUTTING LAYOUT: BIRDIE DRESS (PIECES 1–3)

45 in/115 cm wide

Cutting Layout for Pattern Pieces

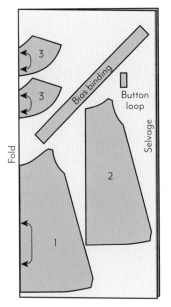

45 in/115 cm wide

PROJECT INSTRUCTIONS

PREPARATION

Download, print, and assemble the Birdie Dress pattern from www.chroniclebooks.com/sundaysews. Cut out the three pattern pieces in your desired size.

1. **Cut the dress**
   a) With Right sides together, fold fabric in half with selvages lined up; press.
   b) Pin the three pattern pieces to Wrong side of fabric, according to the Cutting Layout: Birdie Dress; note that you will need to move piece 3 to cut it twice.
   c) Cut fabric along the pattern outlines.
   d) Transfer all pattern markings to Wrong side of fabric.

2. **Cut the bias binding and button loop**
   a) On a single layer of leftover fabric, (refer to Cutting Layout: Birdie Dress), mark and cut a bias strip 30 by 2 in/76 by 5 cm for neckline.
   b) On the same single layer of fabric, (refer to Cutting Layout: Birdie Dress), mark and cut (on the lengthwise grain) a strip 1 by 2¼ in/2.5 by 5.5 cm for the button loop; set aside.

3. Sew the sleeves

a) Following the instructions on page 27, gather sleeve along shoulder edge, between the two marks (see page 27). Pull both of the bobbin threads so that the total width of the gathering is 3 in/ 7.5 cm. Baste the gathers in place, ¼ in/5 mm from gather's raw edge.

b) Fold over and press long curved edge of sleeve, ⅛ in/2.5 mm to Wrong side. Fold and press this edge again, ¼ in/5 mm to Wrong side. Stitch in place along the inner folded edge (see Figure 1).

c) With Right sides together, align one sleeve straight raw edge with the dress front armhole edge; stitch sleeve to front armhole. With Right sides together, align the remaining sleeve raw edge with the dress back armhole; stitch sleeve to back armhole. Clip the seam allowance (see page 28) of armhole curves and press both front and back armhole seam allowances toward the body pieces. Finish seams (see page 37 and Figure 2).

Figure 1

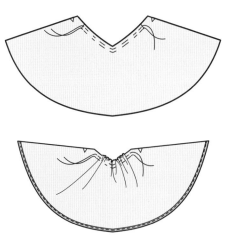

Figure 2

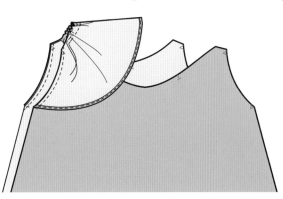

d) Topstitch along entire front armhole on body side, ⅛ in/2.5 mm from seam. Repeat along back armhole.

e) Repeat steps 3a–3d with second sleeve on the opposite armhole.

4. Sew the body of the dress

a) Following the instructions on page 27, gather dress front along neckline between the two marks. Then baste gathers in place, ¼ in/5 mm from neck edge.

b) With Right sides together, align front and back along side edges; stitch seams. *Note:* The sleeves' hemmed edges should not be caught in the side seam stitching. Press seams open and finish seams (see Figure 3).

c) With Right sides together, align back pieces along center back. Stitch center back seam from bottom edge to back opening notch.

d) Press center back seam open, then fold over and press the two sides of the back opening to Wrong side, even with the seam allowance. Finish seams and raw edges of opening from neck edge to bottom edge.

5. Sew the neckline

a) Press neckline bias strip into ½-in/1.25-cm-wide double-fold bias tape (see page 32), then press one end under ½ in/1.25 cm to Wrong side. Re-press the binding creases at the folded-under end.

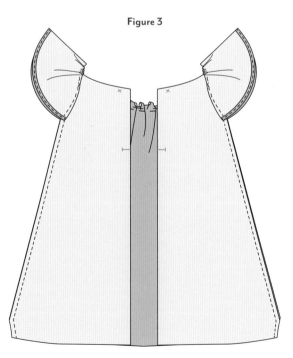

Figure 3

b) Press the button loop into ¼-in/ 5-mm-wide double-fold tape and edgestitch the two aligned folded edges together.

c) Fold the button loop in half, and place it at the wearer's back left neck, overlapping the dress by ⅝ in/1.5 cm. Baste loop in place.

d) Starting at wearer's left back neck, pin folded-under end of bias tape even with the back neck opening, Right side of bias tape to Wrong side of neckline. Aligning the bias tape raw edge with the neckline raw edge, pin around entire neckline, ending at the wearer's right back neck. Cut off excess bias tape, leaving ½ in/1.25 cm beyond the back neck opening. Press this tail of the bias tape end under to Wrong side, even with the edge of the dress. Stitch bias tape to neckline along the first crease from the raw edge of the bias tape.

e) Fold bias tape over to the Right side of the neckline, encasing all the raw edges. Stitch bias tape to Right side of neckline along the folded edge of the bias tape.

f) Stitch along back opening, ⅛ in/ 2.5 mm from edge, starting from the top of bias tape to the bottom of opening, catching button loop. Repeat on opposite side of back opening (see Figure 4).

6. **Finish the dress**

a) Hand-sew button on wearer's right back as marked and slip loop over it to fasten.

b) Fold and press bottom hem under 1¼ in/3 cm and follow the blind-stitch hem instructions on page 38.

Figure 4

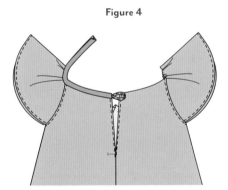

BABY GIFT SET

There's no more perfect gift than one sewn with love. Turn this simple-to-sew set into your new go-to baby shower gift. Light-loft batting and hand-knotted stitches add a quilting effect without the need for laborious patchwork, and the reversible bib can be sewn in only an hour. Quilting cottons are durable even after loads of washing, so expect this gift to last for generations—or at least until baby number two arrives. Roll and wrap the matching set in ribbon to present the perfect keepsake to the mom-to-be.

MATERIALS REQUIRED

Pattern Piece: Baby Gift Bib

Notions: 1¼ yd/1.2 m of batting (¼ in/ 5 mm thick)

1 skein of embroidery floss in coordinating color

1 button (¾ in/2 cm diameter)

Coordinating thread

Fabric and Yardage: 1¼ yd/1.2 m medium-weight cotton (45 in/115 cm wide) fabric for one side of quilt

1¼ yd/1.2 m medium-weight cotton (45 in/ 115 cm wide) fabric for second side of quilt

Sizing: Blanket measures 44 in by 28 in/ 110 cm by 70 cm

NOTES

All seam allowances are ½ in/1.25 cm, unless otherwise stated.

You'll have enough fabric to make two bibs if desired.

CUTTING LAYOUT: BABY GIFT SET

(45 in/115 cm wide)

Cutting Layout for Pattern Pieces

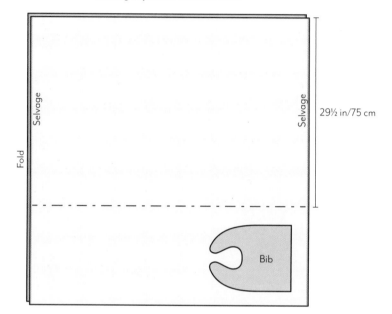

45 in/115 cm wide

PROJECT INSTRUCTIONS

PREPARATION

Download, print, and assemble the Baby Gift Bib pattern from www.chroniclebooks .com/sundaysews. Cut out the bib pattern piece.

....

1. Cut the blanket

a) With Right sides together, align both fabrics. Mark a line 29 in/75 cm from selvage to selvage along the entire width of fabric, according to Cutting Layout: Baby Gift Set.

b) Cut fabric along marking, then cut off selvage edges (about ½ in/ 1.25 cm).

c) Cut a 29-by-45-in/75-by-115-cm rectangle of batting.

2. Cut the bib

a) With the two fabrics Right sides together, pin bib pattern piece to Wrong side of fabric, according to the Cutting Layout: Baby Gift Set.

b) Cut fabric along the pattern outlines.

c) Transfer all markings to Wrong side of fabric.

3. **Sew the blanket**

a) With both of the blanket fabrics held Right sides together, pin the batting to one Wrong side of fabric.

b) Stitch around all four sides of the three layers, leaving a 6 in/15 cm opening on one short side.

c) Clip corners (see page 28), trim excess batting, turn Right side out through opening, and press seams flat.

d) Slip stitch blanket opening closed (see page 39).

4. **Create quilting**

a) Your blanket should now measure 28 by 44 in/70 by 110 cm. If your measurements are different, start your marks at the center of your blanket and work your way out to the edges to keep a nicely balanced look.

b) Use your clear, gridded ruler and marking tool to mark the blanket as follows: beginning 4 in/10 cm from one short edge and holding the ruler parallel to that edge,

Figure 1

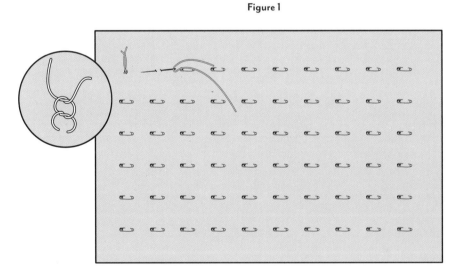

make a small mark every 4 in/ 10 cm across the quilt top. Continue in that same way, making marks in a 4-in/10-cm grid pattern over the blanket. Pin through all layers at each marking (see Figure 1, page 160).

c) Removing the pins as you go, use embroidery floss to make a small stitch, about ⅛ in/2.5 mm long, at each mark. Stitch through all layers and leave about 2-in/5-cm-long tails of floss at each stitch, then tie the tails into a firm knot (see Figure 1, page 160).

5. **Sew the bib**

a) With Right sides together, align the edges of the two bib pieces; stitch around the perimeter of the bib, starting and stopping your stitches at each side of marked opening.

b) Clip along curves and turn right side out through opening. Gently push out corners with a turning tool and press all seams flat.

c) Press seam allowance at opening to the inside and edgestitch (see page 28), ⅛ in/2.5 mm from edge, around the bib.

d) Stitch buttonhole with machine (see page 36) as marked, then hand-sew button on opposite side.

LITTLE HELPER APRON

The mini sous chef in your kitchen will love this bite-size version of the Maker's Apron on page 143. This adjustable smock will protect clothes when their hands get dirty with batter, frosting, or flour. Look for a durable and washable fabric, like this medium-weight cotton oxford, so your little one can wear it for a few years. This fun project will take about as much time to sew as waiting for your cake to bake! Easy-peasy.

MATERIALS REQUIRED

Pattern Pieces: Little Helper Apron, pieces 1–3

Notions: 2¼ yd/2 m of ribbon or twill tape (1 in/2.5 cm wide)

1 yd/1 m of Wonder Tape (optional)

Coordinating thread

Fabric and Yardage: ¾ yd/0.7 m medium- to heavyweight cotton or linen fabric (45 in/115 cm wide)

One Size: Fits children sizes 3–5

NOTES

All seam allowances and bottom hem are 1 in/2.5 cm, unless otherwise stated.

Optional: Skip the patch pocket or use contrasting fabrics to add whimsy.

CUTTING LAYOUT: LITTLE HELPER APRON (PIECES 1–3)

(45 in/115 cm wide)

Cutting Layout for Pattern Pieces

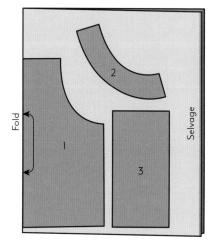

45 in/115 cm wide

PROJECT INSTRUCTIONS

―――――

PREPARATION

Download, print, and assemble the Little Helper Apron pattern from www
.chroniclebooks.com/sundaysews. Cut out all three pattern pieces.

....

1. Cut the apron

a) With Right sides together, fold fabric in half with selvages lined up; press.

b) Pin all three pattern pieces to Wrong side of fabric, according to Cutting Layout: Little Helper Apron.

c) Cut fabric along the pattern outlines, but cut pocket on one layer of fabric only.

d) Transfer all markings to Wrong side of fabric.

2. **Sew the apron and facings**

a) Hem top, side, and bottom edges of apron following the double-fold hem instructions on page 39. Do not hem along the curved arm openings.

b) Double-fold hem each short end of the two facing pieces.

c) With Right sides together, align apron and facing pieces along armhole curves; stitch facing to apron armhole curves using a ½-in/1.25-cm seam allowance (see Figure 1). Clip the seam allowance along curves and press seam open. Fold and press the facings to the Wrong side of the apron.

d) Fold the facing raw edges ½ in/ 1.25 cm to the Wrong side and press. Stitch the folded edge of the facing to the apron about ⅛ in/ 2.5 mm from the inner edge. This creates the armhole casings for the straps (see Figure 1).

Figure 1

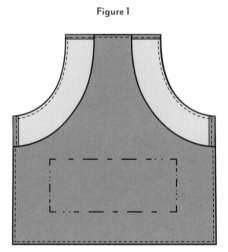

3. **Sew the pocket**

a) Double-fold hem (see page 39) one long edge of the pocket piece, being sure to stitch along this hem. This hemmed edge is now the top of the pocket.

b) Double-fold (see page 39) the sides and bottom of pocket to the Wrong side and press.

c) Use Wonder Tape or pins to secure the pocket in place on apron at pocket markings.

d) Starting at one top corner, stitch around the two sides and bottom of the pocket, ⅛ in/2.5 mm from the folded edge, being sure to leave the top open.

e) Stitch through pocket and apron up center of pocket piece to divide into two pockets. It's easy to create more pockets for pencils, paint-brushes, or pebbles to accommo-date the needs of your mini-maker.

4. **Add the tie**

a) Double-fold hem the short raw edges of the ribbon or tape to prevent fraying.

b) Use bodkin to thread ribbon or tape through armhole casings, starting at the bottom of one side opening, out the top opening, into the other top opening, and back down the opposite armhole casing. You will want to leave a long loop of ribbon/tape at the top for the head to slip through.

c) Wear and play.

SLEEPING BUNNY

A handmade bunny is the perfect companion for a child. Put your basic embroidery skills to work—or pick up a few lessons with this project—by sewing up a cuddly best friend for your favorite kiddo. Girls and boys can be part of the process by making the no-sew pom-pom tail or stitching bunny's sleepy eyes. To make the rabbit even more one-of-a-kind, consider using a print instead of a solid fabric for the body.

MATERIALS REQUIRED

Pattern Pieces: Sleeping Bunny, pieces 1–6

Notions: 1 skein of 6-strand embroidery floss in brown

1 skein of 6-strand embroidery floss in pink

1 embroidery hoop (3 in/7.5 cm in diameter)

Poly-fil stuffing

1 yd/1 m of ribbon (⅛ in/2.5 mm wide)

3 yd/2.7 m of yarn for tail

Fabric and Yardage: ⅓ yd/0.3 m medium-weight cotton or linen (45 in/115 cm wide) fabric for bunny

¼ yd/0.25 m lightweight cotton (45 in/ 115 cm wide) fabric for one side of dress (Fabric A)

¼ yd/0.25 m lightweight cotton (45 in/ 115 cm wide) fabric for second side of dress (Fabric B)

Sizing: Bunny measures 22 in/56 cm from tip of ear to foot

NOTES

All seam allowances are ¼ in/5mm, unless otherwise stated.

Dress is made reversible.

CUTTING LAYOUT: SLEEPING BUNNY (PIECES 1–4)

(45 in/115 cm wide)

CUTTING LAYOUT: SLEEPING BUNNY DRESS (PIECES 5–6)

(45 in/115 cm wide)

Cutting Layout for Bunny

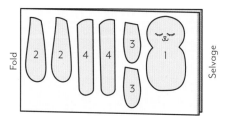

45 in/115 cm wide

Cutting Layout for Dress

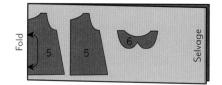

45 in/115 cm wide

PROJECT INSTRUCTIONS

PREPARATION

Download, print, and assemble the Sleeping Bunny pattern from www .chroniclebooks.com/sundaysews. Cut out all six pattern pieces.

....

1. Embroider the face

a) With Wrong sides of fabric together, fold in half with selvages lined up; press.

b) Pin pattern piece 1 (body) to Right side of fabric, according to Cutting Layout: Sleeping Bunny. Using your marking tool, trace pattern and markings onto the Right side of the fabric; do not cut piece yet. Remove pins and pattern. On one layer of fabric only (Right side facing), center embroidery hoop over the face of bunny.

c) With Right side of fabric still facing, use three strands of brown floss (or chosen color) to embroider a running or an outline stitch over marked eyes and a single stitch for each eyelash (see Figure 1).

d) With three strands of pink floss (or chosen color), use a satin stitch to fill in the marked nose and a running or an outline stitch for lips (see Figure 1).

2. **Cut the bunny**

a) With Wrong sides together, fold fabric in half with selvages lined up; press.

b) Pin pattern pieces 2 (ear), 3 (arm), and 4 (leg) to Right side of fabric, according to Cutting Layout: Sleeping Bunny.

c) Cut fabric along the pattern outlines, including the marked pattern piece 1 (body).

d) Transfer all markings to Wrong side of fabric.

3. **Cut the dress**

a) With Right sides together, fold dress fabric A in half with selvages lined up; press. Do the same with dress fabric B.

b) Pin pattern pieces 5 (dress) and 6 (collar) to Wrong side of both fabric pieces, according to Cutting Layout: Sleeping Bunny Dress. The 5 piece cut on the fold will be the dress front and the pieces not cut out on the fold will be the dress back.

c) Cut fabric along the pattern outlines.

d) Transfer all markings to Wrong side of fabric.

Figure 1

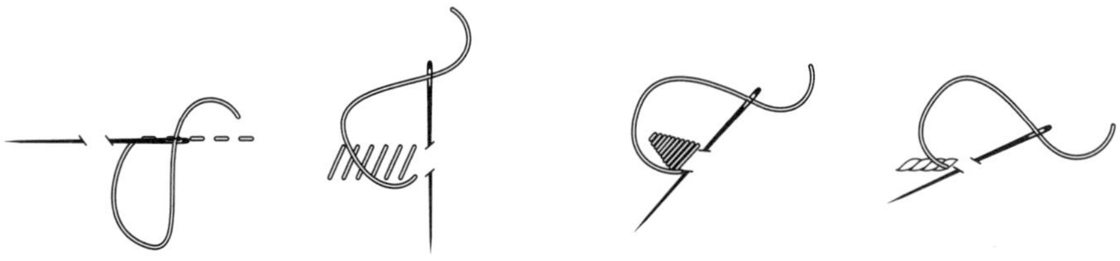

Running stitch   Single stitch   Satin stitch   Outline stitch

4. Sew the bunny

a) With Right sides together, align all edges of one set of ear pieces; pin. Stitch along the long curved edges using a ¼-in/5-mm seam allowance and leaving bottom end open. Turn Right side out through end and press flat. Repeat with second set of ear pieces.

b) With Right sides together, align all edges of one set of arm pieces; pin. Stitch along the long curved edges, leaving end open; clip curves. Turn Right side out through end and press flat. Stuff lightly with Poly-fil. Repeat with second set of arm pieces.

c) With Right sides together, align all edges of one set leg pieces; pin. Stitch along the long curved edges, leaving end open; clip curves. Turn

Right side out through open end and press flat. Stuff lightly with Poly-fil. Repeat with second set of leg pieces.

d) Baste ears, arms, and legs to the Right side of one body piece at the appropriate marks (raw edges together, see Figure 2), being sure to keep these pieces tucked out of the way as you sew.

e) With Right sides together, align all edges of body front and back, sandwiching the ears, arms and legs between the two pieces. Stitch around the perimeter of the body with a ⅜-in/1-cm seam allowance, leaving a 3-in/7.5-cm opening as marked. Be sure not to catch any of the sandwiched pieces in the stitching. Turn Right side out through opening and press body flat along seams (see Figure 2).

173

Figure 2

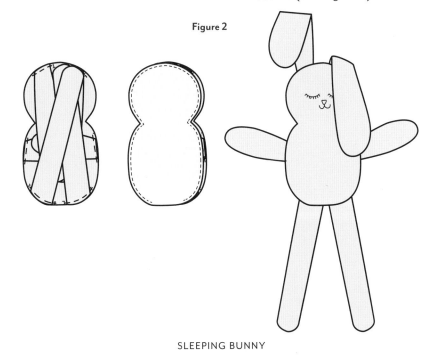

SLEEPING BUNNY

f) Fold and press body opening seam allowance to wrong side. Lightly stuff the body, then slip stitch the opening closed (see page 39).

g) To make the pom-pom tail: Wrap the yarn around three fingers approximately 20 times. Tie yarn ends firmly into a knot around the center of yarn loop, as shown. Trim through all loops and fan ends out to make a tail (see Figure 3). Hand-sew tail to back body.

5. Sew the dress

a) With Right sides together, align one matching fabric set of the dress front and back along shoulders. Stitch shoulders using a ¼-in/5-mm seam allowance.

b) On the same dress pieces, with Right sides together, align side seams on front and backs and stitch.

c) Repeat steps 5a–5b with the second set of dress pieces.

d) With Right sides together, align all edges of collar pieces. Stitch along outside curved edge only. Trim curves as needed, turn Right side out through neck edge, and press seams flat.

e) Find center of dress front neck and align center of collar with this

Figure 3

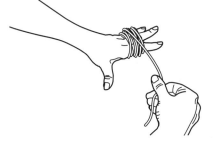

point, Right sides and raw edges together. Place second dress piece on top, Right sides together, creating a sandwich, with all edges matching (see Figure 4). Pin in place and sew a seam along the entire neck edge. Clip curves as needed, then turn dress Right side out and press.

f) Still treating each side of dress separately for folding and pressing, but sewing the two sides together, fold and press armhole seam allowance under toward Wrong side and edge-stitch (see page 38) ⅛ in/2.5 mm from fold.

g) Cut ribbon into four equal pieces.

h) Fold and press under the seam allowance of the dress back edges on each piece toward Wrong side. Place two ribbon pieces between fabric layers on each side, one at the top neck edge and one 2½ in/ 6 cm down from top edge; pin in place. Topstitch back edges closed, ⅛ in/2.5 mm from folded edges.

i) Fold and press bottom hem edges under toward Wrong side. Topstitch hem edges closed, ⅛ in/ 2.5 mm from fold.

j) Slip dress over bunny and tie ribbons closed.

Figure 4

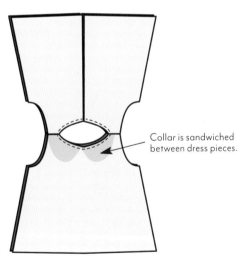

Collar is sandwiched between dress pieces.

ACKNOWLEDGMENTS

I've always said that sewing is a solitary craft, unlike knitting or crochet (it's not so easy to haul your machine to café craft nights). A sewing book, however, takes a village and I'd like to thank the many people involved in the process.

First, thank you to photographer Nicole Hill Gerulat, who not only encouraged me to run with an idea we both had three years ago but also whose amazing talent captured just the right mood and presented the projects in the best light—literally. She also put together a dream team of stylists—thanks to Meg Mateo Ilasco and Mallory Ullman for your fantastic work on the fashion and home front and Janet Mariscal for keeping hair and makeup fresh and fun on our beautiful models, Alexah and Micah. Big kisses to Tessa, the cutest redhead in the Bay Area, who takes direction like a pro while looking sweet as ever in photos. Michelle Pattee's Sebastopol farmhouse couldn't have been a more perfect setting and I thank her and her family for allowing us to turn it upside down for two shoot days.

My editors, Elizabeth Yarborough, Lisa Tauber, and Dolin O'Shea, were wonderful partners in shepherding the manuscript through rounds of solid editing—thank you for your valuable guidance. I'd also like to thank the Chronicle Books design team for a lovely layout. Kelly Williams, your sewing and pattern assistance helped me meet deadlines with ease. Sewing illustrator Missy Shepler, though we've never met personally, was wonderful to work with under tight deadlines—you're a pro! My talented sister, Kristen Grove, came in during the final stretch to pretty up the patterns in Illustrator—thanks, sis!

A big smooch to my daughter Matilda, who was due exactly when the book was due to my publisher, for putting up with a constantly working mom while she lay nestled in my belly. Finally, I'd especially like to thank my love, Ale, for his patience and support during the long process of designing, sewing, writing, and producing a book on nights and weekends for more than a year. Now that we've put this baby to bed, I can't wait to start the journey with our new one.

177

RESOURCES

BOOKS

Here are my favorite sewing books, including a few Japanese selections (now available in English) that I picked up in San Francisco's Japantown, just a few blocks from my home.

JAPANESE SEWING BOOKS

Simple Modern Sewing
By Shufu To Seikatsu Sha

This elegant book offers great variations on basics, from boatneck dresses to A-line skirts to elastic-waist pants.

Sweet Dress Book
By Yoshiko Tsukiori

I particularly love the fabrics and styling in this book. It shows you how to make 23 pretty garments using just six simple patterns.

HOW-TO-SEW BOOKS

The BurdaStyle Sewing Handbook
By Nora Abousteit with Alison Kelly

I love the fit and style of Burda patterns. This book takes you through five of them while explaining how to use sewing patterns.

Vogue Sewing
Edited by Crystal McDougald

This book is a great resource when you're looking to brush up on standard construction techniques.

PATTERNMAKING BOOKS

Building Patterns
By Suzy Furrer

Learn everything you need to know about pattern construction to architect your own clothing.

Built by Wendy Dresses
By Wendy Mullin with Eviana Hartman

This book includes flattering patterns and makes designing every type of dress look easy.

HOME SEWING BOOKS

The Liberty Book of Home Sewing
By Lucinda Ganderton

Make the most of Liberty's beautiful prints with this book, offering 25 easy patterns.

Simple Sewing
By Lotta Jansdotter

I adore Lotta's modern Scandinavian style. This is a great starter book for beginners.

FABRIC RESOURCES

I prefer to shop for fabric in person so that I can test out the fabric hand, but buying fabric online is a wonderful convenience. Here are the brick-and-mortar and online shops that I visited when sourcing fabrics for this book.

B. Black & Sons
bblackandsons.com

This online shop is a great go-to for classic cottons, from crisp shirting fabric to summery seersuckers. If you're in the Los Angeles area, they also have a shop in the city's garment district.

Britex Fabrics
britexfabrics.com

This is hands-down the best fabric store in San Francisco, with four floors of gorgeous fashion and home décor fabrics.

FabricMade
www.etsy.com/shop/fabricmade

Find stripes, checks, and dots in beautiful colors from this online seller.

Joanns.com

The chain store has a great selection of quilting cottons, and their app offers access to amazing discounts.

MissMatatabi
www.etsy.com/shop/MissMatatabi

This Tokyo-based seller has a cute and quirky selection of modern Japanese linen and cotton fabrics.

Purlsoho.com

I refuse to leave NYC without a trip to this fabric store. Out-of-towners can visit its website for a lovely selection of quilting cottons.

The Ribbonerie

This charming shop in San Francisco's Laurel Village has every ribbon under the sun.

Satin Moon Fabrics

Around since the 1970s, this small San Francisco shop keeps its selection of quilting and home décor fabric always fresh.

Spoonflower.com

Choose from loads of fun prints designed by independent artists, or create your own with multiple fiber options.

PROJECT FABRICS

Sunday Sews features fabrics in standard prints (stripes, solids, dots, and checks) that you can find in any fabric store. Here, I've selected the projects with fabrics that truly stand out from the crowd.

Baby Gift Set

Indian Summer by Sarah Watson (Art Gallery Fabrics) with Nani Iro Polka Dot Fabric

Birdie Dress

Nani Iro Fuccra Rakuen Mauritius (www.etsy.com/shop/MissMatatabi)

Lazy Day Skirt

Pure Linen Blue Stripe (www.etsy.com /shop/fabricmade)

Little Helper Apron

Japanese Fabric Heart Bird in Green (www.etsy.com/shop/MissMatatabi)

Matilda Dress

Freeform Arrows in Soft Coral by Domesticate (Spoonflower.com)

Monday Skirt

Ikat: Stella-12 Yellow (Dear Stella)

Pixie Dress

Yoke: Edenham K Tana Lawn (Liberty of London)

Dress: Black and White Check Shirting (B. Black & Sons)

Poppy Tank

Nani Iro Pocho Double Gauze, Red Dot (Purl Soho)

Sleeping Bunny

Dress: Phoebe H Tana Lawn (Liberty of London)

Sorbet Skirt

Kobayashi Linen Blend Spots (www.etsy.com/shop/MissMatatabi)

Spring Clean Tote

Lining: Black Diamonds by Ali Henrie (Spoonflower.com)

Weekend Wrap Dress

Ombré: Daiwabo Collection (E. E. Schenck Company)

ABOUT THE AUTHOR

PHOTOGRAPH BY MICHELLE DREWES

Theresa Gonzalez is the coauthor of the sewing book *Dorm Decor: Remake Your Space with More than 35 Projects* published by Chronicle Books, and is the former editor of the sewing magazine *Cutting Edge*, crochet magazine *Crochet Today*, and knitting magazine *Your Knitting Life*. She has taught online sewing tutorials at NicolesClasses.com and has contributed original projects to *Stitch Magazine*, Apartment Therapy, and Design*Sponge. She lives in San Francisco, California, with her partner, Alejandro, and their daughter Matilda.

Nicole Hill Gerulat is a food and lifestyle photographer with clients in San Francisco and New York City. Her work has appeared in *Real Simple*, *Parents*, *Anthology*, and *HGTV Magazine*, among other publications. She lives in Utah with her husband, Adam, and their two children Evie and Cole.

INDEX